MODERN MAN'S CONFLICTS

MODERN MAN'S CONFLICTS

The creative challenge
of a global society

by

DANE RUDHYAR

PHILOSOPHICAL LIBRARY

1948

Printed in the United States by F. Hubner & Co., Inc.
New York 13, N. Y.

Nothing is more powerful than an idea whose time has come

VICTOR HUGO

Contents

THE BASIC PROBLEMS
OF OUR TIME

❋

HARMONIZING THE OPPOSITES
IN THE LIVES OF INDIVIDUALS

❋

HARMONIZING THE OPPOSITES
IN OUR GLOBAL SOCIETY

✾

✾

The Basic Problems
of Our Time

THE HUMAN NEED

Since the power of the atomic bomb was revealed and the state of active warfare between nations was brought to a standstill, numerous books and essays have been written seeking to outline solutions for the many problems of reconstruction. In practically all of these the emphasis has been placed upon institutions, techniques, legislations—the obsolescence of them, the disintegration of familiar structures, the hope for better ones, the planning necessary to build these new forms of social and economic, political and even religious living. The necessity for outer changes, for new modes of organization, for new types of relationship between nations, classes and social-religious groups is indeed obvious. But what of the *inner* change which alone could make these new structures of society significant, valid, real? What of man himself who is to live in, and to manage these new organizations, these new social mechanisms?

When future historians survey the tragic decades of this century—how tragic, we dare not yet envision—they will say, if they have learnt from history more than we apparently have today, that the failure of our present generations up to this day has consisted in that we have placed our faith in institutions and in techniques of compromise or readjustment, instead of in man himself. Consider what happened to the Roman world after the Punic and the Macedonian wars, when Rome's domination over the Mediterranean regions was all but complete. A new human spirit was in the air. It took form and name in Palestine. But the momentum of the institutions which had been developing for a few centuries—intellectually in Greece, legalistically in Rome—absorbed this new human spirit. Christianity was made in the image of these institutions;

3

Western man was not made in the image of Christ. Rome placed her faith in her institutions—and fell. We too, in America, have been placing our faith in our institutions—and we may fall, in a manner appropriate to our new global world and our atomic age.

The only possibility left to us, and to all our modern civilized world, *not* to fall, is to begin at once placing our faith in man. It is to summon out of the vital and creative depth of human evolution, out of the core of the human spirit, the power to establish a new image of man, in which the respect for the dignity of the individual person is reconciled with the imperative need to establish the fullest possible human productivity.

In this period of reconstruction we face a vast number of crucial dilemmas. We are pulled by opposites. Humanity is in a state of global civil war; and civil war means always a conflict between basic ideologies. Whether they be focused at the political, economic or religious levels, these conflicting ideologies can never be reconciled except through a change in the understanding of what man essentially is. The religious wars of the European Renaissance were in no way essentially different from our present global civil war waged in the name of so-called individualism and collectivism. The terminology used then was as misleading as the one we shout today through the radio lanes of the world. All that was meant was that the evolutionary emergence of a new type of human being had become inevitable, as a result of the release of new powers born of increased human interchange and of new discoveries.

All that is meant today, underneath our tragic and suicidal confusion of voices, is that a new type of human being has become inevitable, for exactly the same reasons. Every new release of power establishes the undismissable need for a new type of human being to handle the vast potential of energy, which, if not used by a new type of men and women, must destroy all men and all women within its radius of action. There will be new institutions, new mechanisms of control, new techniques; but these will prove a blessing to man, *only* if they come as the creation of the new type of human beings, when this new type has definitely established its ascendency over the long ruling "elite" of an outdated society.

Here is the entire world-problem in a nutshell: The democratic reliance upon the individual person must stay; but total productivity on a global scale must be established for all men, and also in all men—thus by all men. The values arising from the five-century old development of nations *as cultural fields for the integration of diverse races,* and superseding those of archaic societies based on the tribal ideal, must be retained in a form purified from political exclusivism and from the fallacy of the principle of absolute sovereignty; *but* atomic power must become the foundation of a global economy and an all-human world-society which will leave no one out and will discriminate against no race, no class, no group.

These two pairs of apparent opposites can only be reconciled as the man of tomorrow harmonizes within himself the still more basic conflict between the ego, structuring his conscious life and his newly acquired sense of individual responsibility as a self, and those powers which, because they are rooted in the usually unconscious depths of man's common humanity, belong, not to the individual, but to Man as a whole.

Harmonization, reconciliation, integration are needed today in every sphere of human endeavor. They are needed in all these spheres *simultaneously.* But the center of the total process of harmonization can only be —the human being. In him, psychology and sociology, atomic engineering and economics, arts and the sciences of management, meet. Man is the measure of all revolutions because he is the only key to everything human. In man, therefore, we must place our faith. And to have faith means here to gain the power to summon forth out of the womb of human futurity the image of the new man, the man whose hands and mind can control the universal energy locked in the heart of the atom, because his own heart has learnt to beat in tune to the ordered rhythm of the universe.

Let us summon forth together this image of the new man, who has the power to establish new goals and the means to reach these goals.

THE CHALLENGE OF TOTAL PRODUCTIVITY

Fire *versus* Seed

It is current practice among historians and archaeologists to divide into successive Ages the millennia during which, according to modern scientific knowledge, civilization developed. These are most commonly known as Old Stone Age or Paleolithic, New Stone Age or Neolithic (beginning anywhere between 25,000 and 10,000 B.C. according to various calculations, and also according to continents), Bronze Age (after 3000 B.C.), and Iron Age (since the time of the Hittites around 1400 B.C., and especially in Egypt after 1000 B.C.) These Ages are not to be understood as sharply defined periods, but as broad and overlapping phases in the development of man's ability to use the products of his environment in order to maintain himself and to further his collective, generic evolution. The selection of typical materials such as stone, bronze and iron as characteristic factors does not imply that the use of these materials was exclusive during the Ages bearing their names, but, rather, that the approach of mankind to the problem of *mastery over its environment* can be conveniently defined in terms of such use.

We underlined the phrase "mastery over its environment" because it reveals the basic meaning of a historical classification which was adopted by the thinkers of a period in which the concepts of "struggle for existence" and of "survival of the fittest" were uppermost in men's minds. Stone, bronze, iron are the substances from which the *essential tools* of culture have been made; and tools are instruments of mastery. As such, they are used in warfare as well as in the production of goods or wares, in the arts and crafts as well as in agriculture. They serve the purpose of man's mastery

7

over other men, over materials to be fitted for efficient use, over the products of the soil.

It is possible, however, to think of the development of human civilization and human mentality in somewhat different terms, and as a result to establish a classification of historical periods on other bases. The archaic Hindu-Greek sequence of "mythological" eras— Golden Age (Satya Yuga), Silver Age (Treta Yuga), Bronze Age (Dwapara Yuga) and Iron Age (Kali Yuga)—the relative lengths of which measure 4, 3, 2, and 1 units of time (each being 432,000-years long) is to be understood as a "spiritual" classification. It was meant to measure, or at least symbolically to characterize, the cycles of deterioration of the creative energy of Spirit, in a cosmic sense—what today scientists call "entropy," the process of "running down" of universal energy. Another classification is one which uses as a defining factor what might be called *man's basic attitude toward production*. Recent events have given to this factor such an outstanding importance that it is essential for all thinking men to realize what it implies, and to grasp the meaning of the profound change which is even now beginning to revolutionize such a basic attitude.

To produce means etymologically "to bring forth." A tree brings forth flowers, leaves and fruits during spring and summer. And likewise the female brings forth a progeny. But this type of production is instinctive and unconscious in the vegetable and animal kingdoms. It remains instinctive and mostly unconscious during the primitive phases of human development. The primitive woman is known to have had—and wherever found today, to have still—an attitude toward the bearing of children very different from that of the more modern woman. The connection between childbirth and the sexual act seems remote to the primitive woman. Pregnancy appears to her as a natural mystery, a seasonal occurrence; and as her sense of causal connections in time is dim, so is the causal relation between the purely instinctive and impersonal act of mating and the slow-maturing change affecting her body. A general connection is obviously recognized; but for long ages it is likely to have been neither a personalized nor a consciously intentional one.

At this earliest stage of human development there is, indeed, no *planning for production*. Man "gathers" what he finds of use to him in his environment. He plucks fruits and nuts; he eats roots, hunts and fishes. In much the same attitude, the tribal group gathers children from the females, when nature produces them. There is no sense of purposeful control over nature or guidance of natural processes. Things happen; and the problem for man is to adjust himself to natural conditions and to survive by taking from the universe whatever is shown to give man strength and the power to increase his number and his chances of collective survival.

This attitude to life of primitive man (as modern history pictures him) became gradually transformed during the New Stone Age. The transformation led to the beginning of agriculture, to domestication of animals, and to the eventual discovery of the wheel and of its uses. But the deeper psychological factor which made these new developments possible was undoubtedly the gradual realization that if certain acts were performed at a certain period, after waiting for what must have seemed a very long time, certain definite, expectable results would occur. This meant the development of what Count Korzybsky significantly named the "time-binding" faculty—a faculty based on memory, on transfer of traditions, and later on the establishment of a calendar and of recorded data, from which eventually generalizations, abstractions and scientific laws arose. This meant the development of long-range purposefulness; thus, of planning.

The growth of such an attitude was furthered by the study of periodical facts in nature, of seasonal changes in the vegetable and animal kingdoms, and of celestial cycles. It crystallized around the study of astrology—the study of the perfect order displayed by the motions of discs and dots of light in the sky, an order so perfect and reliable as to imply that it was the master of the imperfect and not too reliable sequence of natural phenomena on earth. The periodical motion of the sun was seen to affect obviously the yearly cycle of vegetation; the periodical changes of the moon could be referred to the smaller cycles of animal fecundity. These periods became the basis of the calendar; and the calendar, the magical symbol of this new revelation of natural order, the very key to the new human attitude toward life. Man had become a "producer." He lived no longer exclusively by gathering what he found in nature. He set nature to work for him, to increase and multiply what he had found. Man had learnt to use the seed, vegetable and animal. He had understood and was seeking gradually to master nature's power of increase—not only in the fields of the earth, but also in his own nature; in his women and in his psychic nature; biologically and psychically, then mentally; through soil-cultivation and tribal culture.

This great turning point in human evolution, which is now believed by scientists to have occurred some 8,000 to 10,000 years ago, has been symbolized, according to our Western tradition, in the story of Adam and of the Fall from Eden. The Edenic state of human evolution is the state in which men are "food-gatherers." They *take;* they do not *produce* (bring forth). This state is that of the child, who takes from the mother. It is an "infantile" attitude of complete dependence upon the mother—and also, of fear of the mother, when she appears in the form of the "Dark Mother," *Kali,* the Destroyer. It refers to what has been called "the Age of Innocence," when child-like men have neither differentiated individual consciousness, nor "personality," thus no responsibility.

Adam (from the Hebraic root *Adamah,* red earth) is presumably a collective name for a group of men who began to till this red earth in the sweat of their brows after "eating of the tree of knowledge" and being driven from the Garden (Genesis III)—or possibly the name of a traditional personage who led his tribe along this new and revolutionary line. These men, obviously, were covered with red soil while cultivating it with their hands and chipped stone; which may be the reason for the name "Adam." At any rate, at some time, somewhere, the step was taken which led mankind from the Age of Gathering to the Age of Production.

Recent archaeological discoveries seem to indicate that this event of incalculable consequence may have occurred in the region south of Mt. Ararat in the Caucasus, in some of the small valleys of the highlands where the borders of Irak, Persia, Turkey and Soviet Russia meet; perhaps not far from Lake Uzmi and the town of Tabriz, where, in 1850 the great religious leader, called the Bab, was martyred. As the Bab claimed he brought to an end the religious Dispensation which began with Adam (whom he considered as a great Prophet and Divine Manifestation), while heralding the beginning of a new one, this region may indeed have been a peculiarly significant focal point in the development of one phase in human evolution.

Beside the Biblical tradition, another basic myth (found in varied forms in all mythologies) is of great significance in this connection: the Greek story of Prometheus who stole from the gods, fire, and gave it to the humanity he had created—for which act he was chained to a Caucasian mountain and condemned to have his liver devoured by a vulture and constantly growing again, only to be destroyed anew by the sinister bird, symbol of death and of the degeneration of all cycles. The liver was believed by many ancient peoples to be the seat of the soul in the human body. Fire, on the other hand, has been regarded almost universally as the symbol of the spirit and of the "Unknown God," the god of all transformations and metamorphoses; and the repeated rebirth of Prometheus' liver (or "soul") recalls still another myth, that of the Phoenix bird, who, though consumed in the fire at the end of every cycle, is reborn again out of its ashes.

The story of Prometheus seems therefore to hide a promise made to men by some ancient spiritual leader, whom they considered as Father and Liberator, to the effect that, periodically, he would be reborn to suffer with them and sustain them in their tragic progress in the use of the Fire; until the day when a new Age would dawn, and Hercules—the symbolic name of a new solar humanity—having won by his own efforts the spiritual status of "personality" (the Hero state), would free Prometheus from his bondage to the recurrent cycle of life and death on earth, a bondage assumed in compassion for mankind.

Under this mythological symbolism one can readily discover a reference to another great event which, together with the beginning of agriculture, marked a crucial turning point in the evolution of mankind. This event is *the deliberate and conscious use of fire* by man. When it occurred, no one can tell; but it is logical to believe that, while primitive men did use burning wood to warm themselves and eventually to cook some foods as far back as there are any records of human life, the social and technical use of fire for the purpose of *transforming material substances,* and particularly metals, must have come during the Stone Ages—perhaps only after man had begun to cultivate the soil. The making of swords and ploughshares, at any rate, was at first the outstanding application of the new technique; and with it, we enter the Bronze and Iron Ages. However, the softer metals, copper, silver and gold were used before bronze and iron, apparently because their use did not require as much heat, and as good a control of fire.

Agriculture, based on the principle of *seed-increase;* industry, based on the principle of *transformation of matter by man-made techniques*—these two basic activities of mankind characterize essentially what we have already named the Age of Production in contradistinction to the Age of Gathering (the Edenic Age). Agriculture and industry are like two parallel streams running through human history; but their relative importance and the manner in which they have affected human behavior and human mentality—thus society and civilization—have changed considerably since archaic days. Industry has gradually increased its hold upon humanity, seemingly relegating agriculture to a secondary place—at least in terms of essential value or meaning. The city has challenged the farm; the manufacture of industrial wares has grown beyond the production of agricultural products in determining human adjustments to life.

Fire *versus* seed. Two poles of human productivity—and more; for these two controlling factors in the economy of society are also vital symbols for two basic attitudes to life. Both attitudes are present at any time; yet the preponderance of one or the other has profound repercussions upon social patterns and human thought. And today, with the discovery of the use of atomic energy, not only can we foresee the beginning of a new era in production, but, deeper still, the beginning of a new type of civilization and of mentality. The Age which "Adam" opened is coming to a close. The *Age of Seed-increase* is gradually giving way to the *Age of Release of Power*. This is the profound meaning of the Industrial Revolution of one hundred years ago. And only since the year 1945 are we really able to understand what has been taking place; for only since Alamagordo, New Mexico, July 16, 1945, can we begin to understand *the meaning and the full possible use of fire.*

According to classical chemistry fire is the product of combustion; that is, of the rapid oxidation (combination with oxygen) of some material substances—such, for instance, as wood, coal, petroleum. On the other hand, occult traditions in Asia and Europe have considered fire as occurring under three basic aspects; electric fire, solar fire and fire by friction. "Electric fire" was presumably responsible for the first discovery by man that wood (and in general all vegetable substances) could burn, and burning, produce heat and light. "Solar fire" was connected with seasonal changes and the growth of living organisms. "Fire by friction" was the type of fire man could produce—by rubbing together sticks of dry wood—and, by analogical extension, it was related to the sexual act and its bio-psychological effects (impregnation of the seed, warmth of feelings, mental exaltation, etc.).

Electric fire and fire by combustion are understood now to be the results, respectively, of the freeing of electrons and of the shifting of electrons from orbit to orbit within the atom—with a consequent release of energy. In the last few years, however, the nucleus of the atom has been penetrated or smashed. Not only electrons, but protons and neutrons which are far larger than electrons, have been released. Nuclear energy has been set free, as the "binding force" holding together the nuclear particles has been overcome— and this energy is so enormous that, even though only a fraction of it appears to have been released in the explosion of the "atomic bomb," what was released produced an awesome conflagration.

We can now define fire, in a general way, as a release of power sufficiently rapid to produce a noticeable amount of heat, light and rays of all sorts. We can extend this definition to the psycho-mental level and say that fire—"soul fire"—is a release of inner warmth or emotional heat, and of mental illumination. When the Alchemists and Rosicrucians of the Middle Ages worshipped God as "Universal Fire," they paid homage to that ubiquitous and protean Act of Power which releases the energy that coagulates, warms, illumines and destroys all concentrations of matter. That energy, in whatever type of substance it is contained and at whatever level it operates when released, can be called "spirit." It is spirit immanent in material systems—spirit as the essence of universal motion—spirit that binds protons within the nucleus, but also that thrusts through space these powerful particles once the magnetic shell of the nucleus is shattered.

Fire, therefore, is *the release of spirit from material systems*. It is the result of the overcoming of the "binding force," which is responsible for the existence of atoms and molecules, by a disintegrating catabolic, releasing power.* Psychologically speaking, it is likewise the release of the spiritual energy from the bonds of an exclusive focusing on organic living; the release of the soul from the matter-bound desires, and of the spiritual mind from the sense-controlled intellect and selfish ego.

Production, in the conditions of culture and of civilization

Fire *versus* seed means, therefore, release *versus* increase. Production can operate on the basis of both. It can be "production through increase of seed" or "production through release of power—or spirit." It is the preponderance of either of these types of production which constitutes the basic difference between "culture" and "civilization."

A cultural type of society is one which gives a maximum of value and attention to the processes which, at every level of human activity, have as their goal an increase of seed, of concepts, of personal experiences, of bodies and of wares. Culture or cultivation—and also all religious "cults"—refer to the multiplication or expansion of whatever nature presents to man *in a natural organic state.* It is based on the control of the process of organic growth—whether at the biological or at the psycho-mental level.

Civilization, on the other hand, is based primarily on the controlled release of energy and spirit from the substance of man's environment—inner as well as outer. Civilization develops as the releasing process becomes gradually more efficient, more far-reaching, more total. Fire was found in nature. Lightning and solar heat caused forest or grass fires, since the dawn of human evolution on this solid earth of ours. But the *controlled use* of that fire

---

* We may call this power "radio-activity." Hindu philosophers defined it as *rajas* (in Sanskrit the letter and radicle *ra* refers to "fire, heat, love, desire, speed, giving, gold, going, motion, brightness, splendor") The Egyptians worshipped it in the sun as *Râ.* It is also the power that causes the germination of the seed and the emergence of radicles and roots. Strange it is that almost everywhere on earth, men somehow associated it with the sound *Ra!*—a guttural sound produced by a rattling vibration of the glottis and the throat.

(the Promethean gift) marked the beginning of civilization—and of human industry. Wood, coal, oil, gun powder, alcohol have been the main substances in which civilized man has sought for millennia to *accelerate* under control the haphazard or accidental process of disintegration (i.e. release of energy from matter), of which he had found characteristic instances in his environment.

The use of fermented beverages made from fruit-juices or grains is another instance of the way in which man has made the process of disintegration (or fermentation) serve his purpose. In this case the alcoholic beverage was meant to release man's consciousness from the confining routine of an earth-bound existence. Alcohol was given the name "spirits"—or "fire-water"—; its use was not aimed at an increase of organic substance or seed, but at the release of some kind of "spirit" or energy in man. It made men more "spirited." It gave them the illusion of freedom—for a while, and at a certain psychological level. It was a self-induced, easily obtained, foretaste of the true spiritual or mystical experience of liberation—of "psycho-mental radio-activity"—, the key-process to all transcendental states of consciousness.

Atomic radio-activity is simply a further state, a more far reaching and devouring aspect, of fire. It was observed accidentally by the French scientist, Henry Becquerel, studied by the Curies soon after (and now by their daughter and son-in-law) and by the un-officially acknowledged great psychologist-scientist Gustave Le Bon (cf. his book *The Evolution of Matter*, 1905, in which he generalized the concept of radio-activity and of what he called "Black Light"). And now it is being used under control, just as the accidental fire caused by lightning in some primeval forest was used and carefully preserved by primitive man.

Radio-activity occurs in spontaneous form in some material substances, such as radium salts; likewise the slow form of combustion called "oxidation"—and also fermentation and decay—occurs constantly in nature. *Civilization is based on an acceleration and con-*

*trolled use of these disintegrative processes, just as culture is based
on the acceleration and protective guidance of the process of organic
increase of life, especially through seed-reproduction.* For this
reason civilization is consistently dealing with "destructive" or
catabolic forces; while culture deals with "constructive" or anabolic
forces. But these terms, constructive and destructive, are meaningless if an absolute or ethical value is given to them. They have
validity only in so far as they point to the essential character—and
the inevitable dangers—of civilization, of industry, and, today, of
the use of nuclear atomic energy.

Actually the opposition between constructive and destructive
has significance only in terms of organic, cultural and cultual
activities. Within the frame of reference of civilization proper,
and in terms of all spiritual processes dealing with "liberation,"
destruction must be re-named "release." The important fact for
civilization-man in the shattering of the uranium atom is not that
the atom (a material entity) is "destroyed," but that the power held
within the atomic field by the binding force is "released." The
important fact, likewise, for the mystic or yogi seeking at-one-ment
with God or spiritual liberation, is not that the body and ego-
structure of the psyche are shaken, suffer (and in some cases, perhaps, as in religious martyrdom, are destroyed), but that the spirit
held captive within these structures of personality is released.

There are countless atoms; and there are many human beings—
far more today than there ever have been on this earth. Civilization,
as a characteristic attitude to life, concentrates essentially on releasing from atoms (and, in its spiritual aspect, from human personalities) the energy and spirit bound in material entities or organic
structures. It is not "aristocratic," in that it does not deal with
"seed"—always a minority-group. It is "democratic," in that it
seeks to release from every human being the potential spirit locked
or latent in the structures of man's common humanity. Such a
release of the spirit has been the purpose of Hindu yoga, especially

of *Kundalini Yoga,* according to which this spiritual atom in man is imprisoned at the root of the spine and can be released and merged with the universal spirit through a long and difficult process of physical, psychic and mental awakening and control.

All such mystical techniques, practiced in small secret groups in Asia and Europe for millennia, are basically similar to the modern processes for releasing nuclear atomic energy through induced and accelerated radio-activity. They all deal with what the ancient philosopher covered broadly by the term, Fire. Fire is destructive; but so is the superabundance of seeds and agricultural products (as we learnt during the Depression). Likewise, the superabundance of human beings (i.e. over-population) leads to destructive wars for new lands or new markets. Health in any organism means a dynamic balance between anabolic and catabolic forces. Similarly, health in humanity depends upon a dynamic and creative adjustment between cultural increase and the release of energy and spirit effected by the processes of civilization—and we might add, between aristocracy and democracy.

The "Culture of Plenitude" in the Atomic Age

During the approximately 90 centuries since the dawn of the Age of Production cultivation and culture have developed on the foundations of scarcity, thus, of conflict. This was made unavoidable by the fact that agriculture is based on geographical and climateric factors, and that, without the development of industry and the extensive control over Fire (in *all* its modes of expression), man is the prisoner of geography and climate—at the mercy of droughts, storms, floods and pestilences. He is also in a condition of psychological bondage to racial differences, tribal exclusiveness and the "infantile" state of religious dependence upon the Great Ancestor and his successors, shamans or priests.

Exclusiveness results from scarcity—scarcity of food, scarcity of wares and tools, scarcity of mental powers and of spiritual seed (i.e. of creative individual persons). From exclusiveness derive fanaticism, the hatred for the alien and the unknown, and inordinate pride in group-achievements, in one's own religion, race, nation, class—and in one's personal ego. *All typical cultural manifestations have been based so far on scarcity, exclusiveness and the pride of differentiation—on limited productivity, on unhappiness, and therefore on jealousy and ill-will toward some persons and groups of persons.* And the root of all has been fear; fear born of want, lack and of a sense of guilt, fear kept alive in many cases by special groups and organizations which established and maintained their privileges by encouraging this primeval emotion among the masses—then succumbed to it also.

Religions and philosophies have given justification and significance to these facts—for it is their essential function to justify, give meaning, and help humanity to adjust itself to the facts of experience. The blame has been placed upon "human nature," to which was attributed dark and negative characteristics in contradistinction to all the resplendent traits of divine or heavenly Nature. In practice and under the conditions of life to which men have been subjected in the past, these conclusions were sound and valid enough from a subjective standpoint. They may have been necessary in order to palliate and make bearable the pressure of scarcity and anxiety, the shock of constantly repeated catastrophes, wars and famines. Nevertheless, from an objective and absolute standpoint they were entirely beside the point.

Human nature in itself should not have been blamed, but rather the conditions of scarcity under which it was compelled to develop. We do not know "human nature." We know what man becomes when he operates under the law of scarcity—physical, intellectual and spiritual. But we do not know what man will be when *all* men can operate under the law of physical abundance and inner fullness. Fragmentary and temporary conditions of physical abundance in one part of the globe, against the background of generalized starvation, fear and mental confusion in the rest of the world, can give no evidence of what man will become when he is able to operate in total fullness of being, everywhere. The few that are favored by fortune, when the many are in bitter want, are so insecure and fearful of losing their abundance that their unconscious sense of value, their deep life-instincts compel them to regard this abundance as an anomaly, a turn of good luck in a game of chance, something to cling to and enjoy for a brief moment—or else as a God-given gift, which they must defend and retain so as to fulfill some mysterious divine plan. Indeed, the belief in scarcity and war is still so inbred in humanity, so deeply rooted in the collective unconscious of the race, after millennia of justification for that belief, that "human nature" is still its slave. At the very least, it is conditioned by it.

In order to become liberated, collective man must first of all *believe* in abundance, in fullness of being. He must, then, overcome the habits of scarcity, the ghosts of fear and guilt, and repudiate all the institutions and crystallized traditions which not only embody the principle of scarcity, but profit from its application. Man must build a new society in terms of total plenitude of being. He must build it, because now he *can* build it. Today he has the power in his hands; he has the knowledge in his mind; the vision of the future—dim though its outlines may be—has been presented to him by a few inspired seers. And yet, the world over, men hestitate, are confused, are pulled back by memories of failure, by what their learned intellectuals bring forth as precedents, as economic laws, as political inevitabilities. Men are afraid to lose their familiar pittance while reaching for what they are told is just one new phase of the old and unchallengeable natural law.

Ours, nevertheless, is an unprecedented situation. All that man needs is to have the courage to believe it *is* an unprecedented situation, to refuse being dismayed and led astray by the men and the organizations that cling desperately to their ancient privileges.

These had meaning in ages during which the aristocratic principle of seed-cultivation ruled society and man's mastery over Fire was hesitant, limited and insufficient. They have lost whatever shadow of significance the Industrial Revolution had left to them the very day the atomic bomb exploded in the desert of New Mexico.

To say this, however, is not enough. In this Age of Production in which we are living the two factors of culture and civilization, of seed-cultivation and release of Fire, must always develop together and in relation to each other. Man has succeeded in releasing the power that burns at the core of atoms; but release is not enough. There must be adequate "engines" to put to social use, as well as to control, this release of power. By the term "engine" is meant here, not only the material engines of steel—or the mechanisms necessary to control atomic disintegration (graphite, paraffin, lead, concrete) and to confine destructive radiation—; but as well the mental, moral and social instrumentalities which are required for the generalized, constructive and safe use of the new powers in the fabric of society.

Any mechanism or spiritual instrumentality enabling men to control for use the release of any type of power can be called an engine. Man, as controller of energy and as dispenser-manager of power is an engineer. And culture should be considered as the sum-total of agencies entrusted with providing the engines necessary *at all levels* for the social use of whatever kind of energy man has been able to release. Religious rituals and the temples or cathedrals built for their performances are engines for the focalization and release of the collective psychic energy of the people of a community—especially in times when religion is a central determinant in social living. The great myths of a culture, the "prime symbols" defined by Spengler and Jung's "primordial Images of the collective unconscious," the traditional art-forms (such, for instance, as a Sonata-form or a Fugue in music), the yearly festivals and the conventional behavior of a man of culture, the institutions of learning, the academies and the museums, the concert-halls, operas, and baseball games—all these cultural agencies are engines devised so as to control the release of human emotions and collective tensions: engines of a different character than a steam-shovel, a steel-foundry, or an "uranium pile"—but engines just the same, in our sense of the term.

Groups of men operate these various types of engines. They constitute the cultural aristocracy of a society. They control the power and the resources of the society. Until now their controls have been based upon the law of scarcity and privilege. But tomorrow new controls can and must be established on the foundation of abundance for all, of fullness of inner as well as outer being in whoever is able to believe in, to imagine, then to work toward such a state of human plenitude.

This change from a basis of scarcity and privilege to one of abundance and global distribution in terms of the need of each and all represents the great problem of this XXth century. Once effected, a new type of culture will be born, a "culture of plenitude." Not only agriculture but *pleniculture;* not only a cultivation of physical earthly seeds, but the development and increase of the "seed of Man" *through* an ever more abundant crop of mature, responsible and consecrated responsibilities. This global culture of plenitude with roots in the soil of man's common humanity and with stems bearing fruits to the sun of the spirit in Man, was impossible until the Fire at the atom's core was released. There was not enough energy available to animate and sustain it. It is possible today. Every ounce of the earth proclaims this possibility now that every unit of mass has become a womb for immense energy to emerge from, according to the great Einsteinian formula. The global culture of plenitude can be built. It must be built *now.*

Power that is available turns destructive if not released through useful and constructive cultural agencies adequate to handle it. Atomic power can destroy the civilization that set it free, as well as it can energize the mechanisms and organs of a future organic and global civilization consecrated to the fulfillment of Man in all human individuals. We have the power now; how will it be used? What kind of controls shall we build for it? Who shall build them, plan for them, use them—and *for whom?*

The answers to these questions will decide the future of humanity. To refuse giving an answer, is still giving an answer—a negative one, which means that whoever is in charge of the present controls of society and culture today will remain in charge of the new channels for atomic energy release. But these men and groups who are now rulers of our social, cultural, economic, political engines are men trained in the tradition of an age of scarcity; men whose ancestral unconscious is filled with ghosts of cultures dominated by want, fear, greed, lust and pride; men whose intellects are shaped by aristocratic privilege; men whose ability to envision and to believe in the new goals of an Age of total productivity and universal fullness of being for every man and woman that longs for it is almost hopelessly clouded by prejudices and by the fear of losing their position or prestige. These men will not—and in most cases are psychologically unable to—relinquish their hold on the controls of a culture which atomic power has rendered utterly obsolete, after a century of gradual disintegration.

Who are these men? Our politicians, our generals and admirals, our career men, our big business men and financeers, the heads of our institutions of learning and of our agencies for the distribution of cultural works and the spreading of ideas, the heads of most of our clubs and labor unions—and most of our religious leaders. They may be good men, generous men, clever men, very gifted men. But they are men of a system that is based on a now obsolete conception of culture. Their goals are antiquated, at least in their formulation and their modes of realization. They would use and distribute the new powers released by man, the new energies resulting from a globally interdependent humanity, in order to perpetuate that system and these goals—the only ones they know or can "feel" worth while.

In terms of culture, considered as a thing in itself, there is nothing wrong with these men. But culture is nothing in itself. It is not an end. It is only a means to control and to use constructively the powers released by civilization, the spiritual essence freed from material crystallizations. If culture provides controls that fit these powers—whether they be atomic or psychic—and makes use of all the potentialities of human use inherent in them, culture is valid. If culture and the men who operate its engines seek to force the new powers into mechanisms which were developed for and belong to a far less developed and outdated type of energy, then social catastrophes are inevitable. The problem is simple, clear, unavoidable. It is not a matter of sentiment, or of idealism. It is a question of realization and understanding; whether or not humanity is willing to face an issue which renders every other issue secondary, inconsequential and indeed obsolete.

Civilization is not to be blamed if the issue it has raised leads to a catastrophe. It has done its work. The responsibility now rests with the men of culture who operate its controls and who should build new controls to fit the new powers. Civilization is release of power, and power is essentially the capacity to act effectively. Power of itself is neither right nor wrong, good nor evil, constructive nor destructive. What gives it one character or another is the nature of its controls and of the men handling them. If these men cannot grow up to the new requirements set by the new powers available, they become enemies of human evolution. The release of power sets the pace; whoever cannot keep up with it must fall behind. When an entire society falls behind and its leaders seek desperately to force the onsurging power into inadequate engines this society must disintegrate, regardless of whether leaders are well-meaning and their followers good citizens with the best intentions and the most ideal aspirations.

To seek to outline at this time the type of society which will emerge from a culture of plenitude would merely be adding to the number of utopias which have been given form by imaginative and quasi-prophetic men. We cannot know, and it is not important that we should know, how future cities or the future factories will look. In attempting to visualize such finished products of society the imaginative person starts only too often from the things he knows, has suffered from, or fears. The result is a dream-compensation for all the injustices and inadequacies of our period of transition.

What is needed today can be made clear and definite. First, the nature, rhythm and inherent potentialities of the new powers released by modern civilization, at the psycho-mental and ideo-spiritual as well as the atomic-economic level, must be as completely understood as is possible. This is *the one concrete foundation;* there can be no other. Nothing really constructive can ever be accomplished at any time unless the nature of the power necessary for the accomplishment is understood—which does not mean necessarily "intellectually" defined, as intellect (in the modern sense of the term) is also a cultural product, a tool; and new tools for understanding may be necessary, indeed *are* necessary.

However, to understand the nature of the new power, is not enough. To construct new controls, new engines, a new culture for their fullest use is not enough. In fact, it is usually not possible, until the men who operate the old controls have, either succeeded in adjusting themselves to the new rhythm of power, or been removed. And here we face the crux of the social, economic, religious and political problem.

Removal through revolution is a desperate gamble, for revolution in most cases turns into reaction; and even if it avoids this danger it sets into operation dictatorship and mechanisms of external compulsion which tend always to perpetuate themselves long after the crisis of reorientation and their usefulness in it have passed.

Revolution, in its violent aspects, is indeed an expression of scarcity. It implies that the people at large are still so oppressed by lack and fears, so un-awakened mentally and so rigidly controlled by aristocratic mechanisms of social, religious and economic scarcity that they cannot participate in the evolutionary metamorphosis of society except in a purely passive and blind manner. They must, as a result, be forcibly fecundated—violated, one might say—by a small group of utterly determined or passionate men who act as destroyers of the obsolete engines of culture. Through this destruction, seeds are sown, from which new forms, new plans, a new rhythm of existence will in time derive. But these new mechanisms of production will be stamped with the memory of privilege. What one destroys, one always tends to re-embody in one's own tomorrows. The new forms differ; the spirit within them may tragically reveal the ancient ghosts in control of new bodies.

What, then, is the solution? Essentially it is the appearance of men and women who, because they realize the crucial need of the times with utmost poignancy, consecrate themselves utterly as potential channels of expression for the answer of the spirit to this human need. Spirit always answers all vital human needs; it is, by definition, that which fecundates the "dark waters of chaos" with a creative Ray. We may refer it to evolution as understood today; speak of it, with Bergson, as the *elan vital*—or we may consider it as a creative influx, a Pentecostal Fire, emanated from God and reaching an Apostolic Brotherhood united in mind, in consecration and in purpose. We may speak of a new "mutation" operating through individuals of genius who are like "sports" among men—or we may prefer to think of a creative act of God *through* consecrated individual persons whose minds and hearts have become crystal-clear, as lenses to focus and give form to the divine inspiration.

In either case, there are the few men of vision and the masses; the potential fecundator and those who need fecundation—and seeking to thwart or destroy the new seed, there are the privileged groups, the men at the controls of a dying society, the minds filled with traditions and with ghosts . . . some of whom may uneasily readjust their thinking to the new realities of power; most of whom rigidly fight to the bitter end against the *inevitable* rise of a culture of plenitude.

It is "inevitable," now. It may be delayed, but it must come, because the power that has been released *needs* adequate engines to express itself. Evolution is not reversible. Humanity slides back, but whatever man has released, man will learn to use. Power and the use of power are two phases of one single reality. Man may shrink from using it and let power seek destructive paths of least resistance; but that power which man has released, that very same power man must sooner or later come to use adequately. As power is released there is always some man or group of men who gains the understanding of its use for collective human purpose—to the end that Man be fulfilled. It is these men that count. They constitute the spiritual seed of humanity. Only the seed knows what to do with the power of life.

There are such men today; all over the globe; in all walks of life; eager to give out their understanding, the ideo-spiritual seed from which a new culture of plenitude and a new society will gradually emerge. But they are not enough. Not only should there be many more of them, but there must be among the people of the world the *expectancy* of their coming, the eagerness for them, the readiness to be fecundated by them into a new birth of culture. The more poignant this expectancy of the common man, the more focal the demand for a solution to the problems which the atomic bomb and the global interdependence of all nations have posed and which mean life or death to him, the greater the faith of all awakened individuals in Man, in Life or in God—the more powerful, the more creative will become the voice of the few who have vision and the courage to assume the responsibility of its formulation.

A challenge is upon mankind: the challenge of maturity and of total productivity. It is directed to the individual person; it is directed to society at large. It is one challenge. Every man must meet it.

THE TRANSFIGURATION OF THE CONCEPT
OF PERSONALITY

A man's life is stamped with the character of his most basic desire. A society, a culture, a civilization are likewise moulded by the dynamic striving of their collectivities after some goal to which their prophets, geniuses and heroes give expression. Patterns of social behavior and of political organization, religious and cultural ideals, customs and fashions are unified at root by this collective drive. Individual men and women are impelled by it. It constitutes the substance of their "collective unconscious." Though they may be but dimly aware of the full implications and meaning of the fundamental urge seeking within them all to emerge from latency to clearly formulated actuality, yet they are forever ready to respond eagerly to whomsoever gives it utterance in symbols and in deeds.

Individuals are born and die. Cultures and societies rise and disintegrate. But, within all men, a few fundamental instincts, faculties and aspirations keep on developing with varying emphases, ever striving toward their fullest possible realization within the context of the physical environment provided by the earth-surface and its changing climates. These fundamental potentialities and facts of human nature constitute "man's common humanity." The common humanity of all men is that which unites all men by the roots. But all roots have sprung from seeds; and the power which is in the root forever seeks to ascend toward the sun and, in combination with the sun's light, to reproduce that seed from which it once emerged.

Man's common humanity is made up of all the factors which at the psycho-mental and anatomical-physiological levels can be said to be characteristically "human"; which therefore represent, either

29

the new departure in evolution (according to the "scientific" viewpoint) or the archetypal seed-image sown by a divine Power, or Powers, into the soil of the earth. Whatever way one explains their appearance, these specifically human characteristics should be considered symbolically as, both, seed and root. They are *seed-potentialities,* and at the same time they are permeated with, and able to release, a *root-power* which energizes the one great multifarious effort of the human race toward the actualization of its basic seed-potential. This effort takes many forms and directions. Infinitely varied are the avenues of expression devised by the leaders of men—individuals who, having envisioned some new aspect of man's common potential and translated the vision into a goal, radiate upon their fellowmen the contagious desire to attain this goal. Yet, at the core of all these strivings and ideals, of all these paths of individual and social development, of all the religions and cultures of the ages, there is one ineradicable and inexorable drive impelling humanity toward a single universal goal. This goal is the fulfillment of man's common humanity in "personality," *the complete and total actualization of the seed-potential of humanity.*

Whether one believes in an emergent or a purposeful evolution, or one thinks of humanity as the matrix from which individuals emerge, eventually to manifest, according to a divine "Plan," the perfect likeness of a creative God or gods, the universal evolutionary process can readily be understood by most thinkers as a drive toward greater fulfillment and an ever more complete realization of wholeness or perfection. Where there is no accord, however, is on the point of what constitutes fulfillment and perfection for man; nor can philosophers and religious leaders agree upon a method for the attainment of this goal. As a result the word "personality" has been given a multiplicity of meanings, and our task now is to establish the meaning and purpose which the new society in the process of global formation should give to the individual person, if it is to deal constructively and spiritually with the new powers now ready for use.

The basic meaning of personality

Etymologically, the term comes from the Latin "persona" (*personare;* to sound through) which refers to the masks worn by the actors in Rome as well as in Greece. Masks have also been used in one form or another in all primitive cultures. They are still used today in many parts of the world, for instance by the American Indians; and a clear understanding of the essential reason for their use in various historical periods enables one to realize the meaning of personality in all that the term implies.

A contemporary school of thought (particularly along the lines of Theosophy, New Thought and popular psychology) stresses in its use of the word the modern emotional connotations of the term "mask" (*persona*) and thus concludes that the human personality is indeed "nothing but" a mask for the real man, the "individuality"—the spiritual entity which, it is assumed, is immortal and indeed a "spark of divinity." Also, Carl Jung, the great Swiss psychologist, has used the Latin term "persona" to define that portion of the human being, whose function it is to establish a successful adjustment to the demands of society and of the professional life, and which often crystallizes into a rigid mask-like entity. The Jungian "persona" is a kind of "partial personality," compensated for by the complementary development of the "anima" (or in the woman, "animus") which represents man's attempts to adjust himself to the demands of his inner life and to the puzzling, irrational emergence of unconscious psychic factors (dreams, fantasies, vague yearnings, moods, etc.).

However, in his later books, Jung—while retaining the above-described concept of the "persona"—gives the very broadest possible and most positive meaning to the term "personality," making it encompass the ideas of "fulfillment, wholeness, a vocation performed, beginning and end and complete realization of the meaning of existence innate in things." And he ends his major work *The Integration of the Personality* with the statement: "Personality is Tao"—Tao being, in Lao Tze's philosophy, the universal and ultimate creative Essence as well as the "way" toward the harmonic fulfillment by man of the total implications of being.

During the last decades, a school of philosophy has developed, in America and in Europe, which has assumed the name of "Personalism." A personalist is usually a man who considers the human personality as an ultimate and quasi-absolute entity and as the one valid goal of human existence. He therefore refuses to make personality subservient to the demands of any larger social whole— such as the State. According to Personalism, all things in society (and perhaps in the entire universe) are made for, and should concur, to the realization of one ultimate purpose: the fulfillment and perfection of the individual person.

If, however, this understanding of the meaning of personality is accepted, how can it be reconciled with the etymological significance of *persona,* the actor's mask? The reconciliation can be effected if we consider not the modern feeling-attitude toward the "mask," but instead the magical purpose of the archaic masks in sacred rituals, and later in the theatrical performances of early Greece. For us, moderns, to be masked is to hide one's true, vital identity under a fictitious, or at least a partial character. But when the Hopi Indian wears the sacred mask of a god, when the Shaman of Asia covers his face with the conventionalized representation of the tribal Totem, these priest-actors are not *hiding* their individual nature; they are *glorifying* themselves by identifying themselves with the effective creative power—the *mana*—of a superhuman or elemental being.

They have, in fact, no "individual personality" to hide! They hardly consider themselves as individuals, in the modern sense of the term. They are functional parts within a, to them, real and concrete organism: the tribe—which in turn is felt, in most cases, to be one with a living universe. If then the tribesman becomes entitled—as part of his tribal function—to wear the mask of a god and to enact ceremonially the god's vital attributes, what happens is that he assumes a universal and creative role. He performs god-like acts, magical acts. He becomes identified with the god in so far as the god acts out his divinity. Likewise, the Christian priest who celebrates the Holy Mass enacts, by virtue of his consecration and of the age-old transfer of the spiritual (magical) power of the Christ, the sacrifice of Jesus. When he puts on the consecrated vestures he is not less-than-individual; he becomes an active and efficient symbol of the divine Incarnation. He performs the works of Christ; not only in the name of Christ, but (at least in the case of the Pope) *as* Christ.

The sacred rituals become in time the repeated performance of the deeds of the great tribal Hero. Then also the actor who puts on the mask revealing the countenance of the great Personage identifies himself with his heroic and spiritual essence; while, stirred by the magic emotion of the performance, the men of the tribe feel themselves more tangibly united in their primordial seed-nature (as sons of the tribal Ancestor). They are stirred into more unified actions by the tribal root-power released in them—or as Jung would say, by the dominant "archetype" of their collective unconscious. At this stage, the purpose of the performance has already reached the psychological level; indeed it is a blend of the magical and the psychological. Soon the latter will become the dominant factor. Greek philosophers will consider the tragic performance as a collective act of *catharsis* (emotional purification or purgation).

The actor's mask—the "persona"—portrays an emotion in its essential, magnificent or awesome, character. Whoever wears that mask—and whoever opens his soul to the impact of the power-releasing performance—is made to live at a pitch of intensity which he has become too weak to sustain in his humdrum existence, or too intellectualized to welcome without fear. The root-functions of his psyche are violently stirred; and this cathartic action parallels in the psychic realms that of purgative substances whose function it is to stimulate the torpid liver and other digestive organs into enhanced activity. Indeed all rituals are conceived, ever since the dawn of humanity, as magical means *to induce a renewal or an increase of activity.*

It is in the light of this fact that one must understand the significance of the statement by medieval philosophers that personality is the attribute of God—and of God alone. Personality is then conceived as the equivalent of divine Sonship—a vehicle for the creative power of the godhead. Christ is the Only Begotten Son of the One Father; therefore there is but one Personality in the world, which is Christ's. When the priest puts on the "sacred vestures" of his office (symbolizing the "Robe of Glory" of the Christ) he assumes this divine and unique character of personality. He performs, in such character, the works of God—the eternal trans-substantiation of matter and the redemption of Adamic, earth-conditioned, sinful man.

When the Christian Middle Ages faded into the Renaissance and the crystallized formalism of the Classical Era, when Louis XIV set himself as Solar King (*"le Roi-Soleil"*) and identified his person with the State (*"L'Etat c'est moi"*), when the doctrine of "kingship by divine right" was promulgated by the totalitarian rulers of the XVIIth century (*"Le Grand Siècle"*) the concept of personality became precipitated upon the shoulders of kings—then, of princes—finally, of the great bourgeoisie of the industrial and commercial XIXth century. The atomization of personality was the great event of Romanticism.

Romantic culture is the culture of the individualized personality —the worship of every man: every man a priest of God; every man a king unto himself and his world; every man, a Son of God in so far as he performs God's works, that is, as he acts out personality, the one creative divine attribute. In the basic and traditional sense of the term, therefore, to have personality is to act out the divine Sonship immanent in every man by virtue of his being born a human being. It is to manifest, effectively and in deed, the mysterious fusion of "human nature" and of "divine Sonship" which is what the Christian mystic means by the Incarnation. But while the Catholic Church, and its modern Neo-Thomists, believe in *only one Incarnation* — thus, in only one Personality, Jesus-Christ — through which alone an inherently sinful "human nature" is redeemed and made to partake in divinity, the philosophy of Personalism claims that every human being is, potentially at least, such an Incarnation. He is so, because the concept of "man's common humanity" carries no implication of sinfulness or absence of spirituality, but instead includes an immanent and primordial spiritual essence—a God-seed. This means that in every human being spirit, mind and matter are inherent, consubstantial and interwoven; that therefore, in every human individual, the wholeness of universal being *can* be demonstrated, acted out—which is the fullness of personality.

Spirit and Personality

Medieval Christian mystics had spoken of the "immanent Christ"; medieval occultists and alchemists had called every man a potential "microcosm," a small but all-inclusive replica of the universal Whole, the "macrocosm." The roots of personalism are deeply embedded in the mental soil of European culture, and indeed in a Christianity that has stressed and still believes in the essential dignity of the human person. However, one should differentiate between two attitudes which, while they give to personality the same practical meaning and validity, nevertheless conceive in different ways its ultimate position in the universe and in relation to God. In a sense, one might say that the distinction between these two approaches to personalism parallels the philosophical and basic difference between Catholic and Protestant Christianity. In both cases the essential nature of the contrast may be said to reside in the placing of an emphasis upon either a *universalistic* or a *pluralistic* conception of spirit.

In its extreme form the universalistic emphasis leads to the Catholic belief that only in Jesus-Christ divine and human natures have ever been, or will ever be integrated in the total and supreme manifestation of personality; that therefore the one great spiritual Act has been performed once for all by Christ, and men can only partake reflectively in, or imitate and "prolong" this Act which is the central fact of the entire universe. On the other hand, the pluralistic emphasis leads to a type of "monadism" or spiritual atomicism, in which every personality is considered as an absolute and an end in itself, even though it operates within the context of accepted and fulfilled social relationships. And while this monadism is not to be confused with the chaotic or "rugged" individualism of the so-called "democratic" society of our days, or even more of the American Frontier days, nevertheless the former may be said to retain some of the basic characteristics of the latter.

The problem which the personalist who believes in spiritual pluralism must face is how to define spirit or spiritual activity in a consistent manner. Spiritual activity can hardly be regarded as anything but an essentially integrative type of activity. Even when spirit appears to act as the Destroyer of obsolete forms the purpose of such acts is to release frozen units for re-integration into a vaster whole. Personality itself is the result of many and varied kinds of integrative processes. In the "holistic" concept of evolution presented by Jan Smuts, the genesis of personality is shown to be the last in a continuous series of whole-making operations. It is spiritual in as much as it manifests the most inclusive and most coordinated type of integration which universal evolution has produced.

Can we stop with personality and force ourselves not to imagine any further development of the universal integrative process? Must we conceive of some extra-cosmic God or some evolutionary power that, having produced the human person, had no more integrative energy—no more "spirit"—to use, and let thereafter a spiritual entropy prevail? Is the fulfillment of personality in man the ultimate spiritual fact, and should the universe of spirit be pictured as a multiplicity of perfected personalities?

The personalist, it is true, would not consider these personalities as isolated, and still less insulated, individuals. He would undoubtedly realize that they have emerged from some common matrix, social and biological, and that they have formed themselves through a constant inter-relatedness of activities, from which what Carl Jung calls the "process of individuation" derives its substance and its basic symbols common to all men. The personalist might agree to picture symbolically these personalities as "seeds" which have emerged from the web of complex organic relationships constituting the vast plant of society. Each personality-seed is complete in itself; each has gathered to itself the experience of humanity in freedom and creative interplay.

However, to say that all these seeds, each by itself, is an end in itself and an absolute value seems indeed to stop short of the goal of spiritual understanding. One step is left to be taken: the realization that every seed born within the vast expanse of the great tree of man's common humanity is a manifestation of the "seed-hood" of humanity. The seed of wheat does not live for itself, but as a witness to the creative power, significance and immortality of Wheat. The individual human personality, likewise, has ultimate spiritual meaning as an expression of the creative power, significance and immortality of Man. The true life of personality is a life of utter service to Man. An integrated and fulfilled personality is an individualized incorporation of Man.

The capitalized term "Man," thus used, is synonymous with "divine Sonship." Spirit is one, and Man is one—personalities are many. They are varied in their characteristics and in the forms which their creative power takes as it expresses itself in answer to the need of the time and of the place in which such a release of spirit occurs. Personalities are varied in that they define Man *in time and space* by the limits they impose upon Man's powers. Yet except that Man lives and acts through a human person, this person has not attained the spiritual status of personality. Man is the unity of all perfected personalities. This unity constitutes the seed-hood of humanity, the beginning and the consummation of human evolution.

In this conception of personality nothing is subtracted from the spiritual value and the essential dignity of the human person. The plurality of spirit is recognized in terms of the fact that spirit manifests always in answer to a need, and that to the variety of material conditions and needs a corresponding plurality of spiritual characteristics must answer. Yet the unity of spirit is also realized. That all concrete personalities have the same roots is an evident fact of biology and psychology. But humanity is not only a unity below the conscious level. Roots originate in seed. This seed-unity is a spiritual potentiality to be actualized in a more inclusive manner through and at the innermost core of all personalities that have reached fulfillment, and in so doing have recognized themselves as separate manifestations of Man. Each separate manifestation is rightly a law unto itself; but only *in so far as the personality accepts and acts out completely its inherent participation in Man;* that is, in so far as it performs the "works of the Father," the works of the spirit. In so far as man acts as a "Son of God" he is an avatar of Man. The "mask" he wears is the signature of his consecrated response to the need of humanity at the time and place of his life-performance. In his acts he is differentiated by this particular "need" —and this constitutes his limitations. But, at the core of his being, the "seed of Man" is growing, maturing; until the day when, having fulfilled his service to humanity and society, all else but this "seed" will fade away. This seed is *an organism of spirit;* it does not die. In essence, it is Man, the one Son of God; and yet it is also the concentrate of the experiences of the many individual personalities, from whose stems it grew. One Soul, but many differentiated mind-egos: unanimity, but also individual freedom—such is the reality of the spirit, as far as the human consciousness can reach.

The tragedy of official and dogmatic Christianity is that it refuses to accept any Incarnation of divine Sonship save that which occurred in and through Jesus-Christ. Other religions of the Near-East (Manichaeanism, Islam, and recently the Bahai Movement) teach that such divine Incarnations occur before the beginning of every Age, or cycle—in the persons of Prophets and Messengers who alone manifest God and alone are intermediaries between God and sinful men. Personalism claims, however, that every human individual can be a Son of God—or more accurately, that every human being is, *in potency,* a Son of God. In potency only; until the day comes when, through his own regenerative and creative efforts, the individualized human being attains the fulfillment of personality. The power of the Root surges forth in man's common humanity; is therefore active in every human being. But the Seed forms itself anew, in concreteness of spiritual substance, only at the core of the total, integrated personality: and this is what the mystic calls "the birth of the Living God." The God-seed emerges from latency to actual manifestation in the individual who, having accepted the fullness of his responsibility to humanity, discharges it in dedicated service and in active participation in the life of society.

Two kinds of participation

Every man who is not a completely isolated individual participates in some manner in the life of his environment. But the character of a man's participation in the activities of society and of the universe can be of various kinds. Each type of participation defines essentially the spiritual status of the man. Likewise the ideal of participation generally held by a social group or culture establishes the spiritual character of this group or culture.

The general philosophy of personalism insists that every human person is entitled to a type of participation in which the integrity of the personality is safeguarded by society. While it considers the "individual" as an atom which has significance and value only in terms of its being a part of a particular whole to which he "belongs," it regards the "person" as an integral whole, as a microcosm, entitled to free decisions and to the pursuit of what Carl Jung calls (in his book *The Integration of the Personality*) his vocation. Indeed it is in its protest against the collectivistic totalitarianism of the modern State or Church that contemporary personalism—especially in Europe — finds its most forceful expression and *raison d'être*.

However, if we take an historical and evolutionistic view of the matter, we cannot fail to realize that no human being is born with the characteristic attributes of personality. Whether in the tribal state, or today in childhood, man has to win his personality. Personality is an emergent state. It implies at first a long process of differentiation (the emphasizing of all that makes one different from others), the gaining of a conscious and objective attitude toward oneself and others, a weighing of motives and goals, the acquisition of tested values—and finally a process of integration and consolidation.

If a whole civilization becomes polarized by such a process of individualistic differentiation, the outcome can only be a generalized accentuation of intellectual analysis, competitive faculties, soul-dissatisfaction with the norm, and spiritual restlessness. This leads, on one hand, to a great development in acuity, analytic power and inventiveness of the mind of ever-farther-seeking individuals—thus modern science and technology—and, on the other hand, to a thorough intensification of the multi-headed hydra of selfishness, greed and lust for power, nurtured by fear, loneliness and insecurity.

Combine the positive results of the scientific and self-emancipating mind with this monster, and you have our modern civilization and its "atomic bomb." You have universal skepticism and the wholesale degeneration of all communal (and indeed "human") values. You have the Jazz Age, with its utter selfishness, its mental superficialities, its maudlin sentimentality and aimless sexuality. This, inevitably, arouses a compensatory trend; a *blind aggregative* compulsion. It must be "blind" because the substance of vision has been frittered away in centrifugal social, religious and cultural dissociation—and in peripherical sexual abnormalities or hyper-excitation. It is a "compulsion," because it implies a revolt of the unconscious against an exclusive focusing upon consciousness, a revolt of the irrational root-instincts against the dried up rationalism of an over-jealous and exclusivistic "scientific" spirit. It is "aggregative"—i.e. it implies mass-hypnosis and the agglomerative snowball technique—because it is a violent reaction to an extreme of individualistic self-expression unrelated to any communal or cosmic frame of reference.

Thus, Fascism is born—and a virulent, hypnotic kind of mechanized tribalism, the Nazi regime. Thus also the great religious matrices of the past are given renewed strength and modernized "spiritual" justifications by confused individuals seeking a psychological-spiritual "return to the womb"—and new ones are formed. Under the category of "religious matrix" one should include the Communist Party of Lenin and Stalin, because of the rigorous and impersonal attitude it fosters upon its adherents, because of its dogmatic approach and its resemblance to a militant theocratic organization. Economic materialism and atheism can be the substance of a religious attitude if enkindled by a fervent and even fanatic belief that the Cause is dedicated to human betterment and redemption from social evils, that it is an expression of the "need of the

times" and of an evolutionary surge toward higher human goals.
And where this attitude develops in an atmosphere of "mental
scarcity"—that is, among races and classes long held in ignorance,
poverty and illiteracy, and thus unable normally to develop personality—the almost unavoidable result is that a minority-group, pos-
sessing definitely needed and timely attributes for dynamic leadership, is compelled by the very force of circumstances to emerge as
a kind of priesthood, religious Order or consecrated Brotherhood.

The rule of such a group can be called a matrix-rule, in the sense
that it aims at moulding a new culture, at setting forth new values
with dogmatic, compulsive and "magical" power. Modern totalitarian propaganda is a modernized form of magic, and the element
of fear and the menace of invisible hovering death are not foreign
to it. It does not mean that there is not an element of freedom and
democracy in the Communist State; but it is freedom and democracy *within the set framework of a dogma, or ideology.* If one is
born into this social-cultural framework and if one seeks only to
fulfill its postulates, its goals and its archetypal structures, then
there is great richness of living, of faith, and of accomplishment
in store for the individual. However, the goal of the system is to
build a collective cultural whole or organism—a "body"—in which
human beings act as cells bounded by a rigid skeleton and by set
patterns of metabolism, *as functional parts but not as wholes-in-
themselves* (that is, personalities).

Such a system was in force in the Catholic Middle Ages, especially during the centuries when the Church reached the apex of her
power. These centuries saw the rise of the magnificent Gothic Art,
and the culture they produced was in a sense far greater than that
of the much publicized and much over-rated Classical Era. The
Gothic society had tremendous vitality, faith, enthusiasm, creative
power, eagerness for knowledge—and it knew freedom of a sort.
Not freedom to become an independent individual and to develop
personality as a spiritual fact *outside of* the organic structure of so-

ciety; but the freedom to fulfill a particular (and, normally, an inherited) function in the social organism, in deep emotional security and with a maximum sense of functional productivity and participation.

Such a participation, however, is not the kind of participation
which the personalist philosopher regards as consistent with the
character of personality. It is an *organic* kind of participation which
does not start from the individual person as a spiritual foundation,
but rather which utilizes individual molecules of humanity to build
a collective organism. Organic participation means participation
as part of an organic whole which is born and which will die, with
no possibility for the participant to reach beyond the cycle bounded
by this organic beginning and end. It is the type of participation
which can be symbolized by the function of the *leaf* of the plant.
The leaf cannot reach beyond the plant; it cannot stand alone, nor
have meaning of itself and in itself alone; it must die with the disintegration of the plant. A particular leaf has value only in terms
of a particular plant, within which it serves a definite purpose—
even though the purpose might be modified and the green leaf transfigured into the radiant petal of the flower.

The *seed,* on the other hand, can stand alone. It carries its
own meaning. Even though it was grown from the plant and existed
as a functional part of the plant, the seed can—and indeed it *must*
—become liberated from the plant, if it is to fulfill its seed-des-
tiny. Nevertheless, the seed is not an isolated whole. Though de-
tached from the plant, it actually participates in that of which the
plant itself is an expression. It participates by being free from a
particular plant—its mother or matrix—; because this freedom is
the pre-requisite for another kind of participation in a greater reality—the species. And this new participation, born of freedom, implies not only an inner bondage to the future plant, but sacrifice—
the sacrifice of all seeds to the new vegetation. This sacrifice is
demanded of the seed by the species, whose essential and ultimate

purpose it must serve in total self-surrender *as a condition for being significant and valuable as a seed.*

Root, leaf and seed are symbols; and obviously what has been said of them must not be taken too literally. But they are most potent and meaningful symbols. Indeed this distinction between two kinds of participation, symbolically called here "leaf-participation" and "seed-participation," is fundamental. The participation of the leaf in the activities of the whole plant is "organic," in as much as it is, both, defined and bounded by the circumference—in space and time—of a particular plant's life and destiny. The participation of the tribesman in the tribe, of the medieval craftsman in the communal creation of the Gothic cathedral—a cultural organism—, and (in an at least relative sense) of the average Soviet citizen in the collectivistic and Party-ruled society, is of the same order. It is "leaf-participation," organic participation.

On the other hand, the type of participation demonstrated in the life of a creative person who (though having matured within a particular nation and culture) has found his ultimate significance and destiny in his service to the whole of humanity, and (though being the ultimate product of a particular soil and root) has established his home on any and all continents—this, indeed is a *spiritual* participation. It is the participation of the "seed-man" in the total life of humanity, past, present and future.

The seed-man has reached freedom from a particular race and culture, freedom from particular human and geographical conditions—but *only* in order to assume consciously and willingly the bonds of his total responsibility to Man. He has become identified, consciously and deliberately, with the onward surge of human evolution; or, we might as well say, with the "Will of the Father," or with "God's Plan." He is most bound where he is most free. He is bound futureward; while the "leaf-man" is bound pastward. Free from the pull and the compulsion of the past (the root), he is *spiritually* bound, together with his companion-seeds, to the future of Man. Just because he is fulfilled in personality he must die into Man, but this death is immortality, for that with which he becomes thus identified is "divine Sonship." It is God-in-act.

The seed-man loses the limited features of his being, as, having reached the fullness of personality, he becomes identified with the "mask" of God—the Son. Yet, even though the words uttered are those of the cosmic Poet, the voice that rings through that "mask" is the seed-man's own voice. And even though he is one with all seed-men that were, are and ever will be—and they together are the many "masks" of Man—, yet his "Name" is forever remembered; because it is a link of power and of significance in the immortal thread of Man's destiny, a noble deed recorded for all ages in the great Book of the Living Civilization, which is God's masterpiece.

Is, then, personality (in its deepest, most vital and most spiritual sense) to be regarded as an ultimate, an end in itself; or as a means to some greater end? It is *both*. It is an end which consciously and deliberately assumes the responsibility of participating, as a symbolical "seed," with all other personalities who, together, constitute the path to, and the substance of a universal Purpose and a universal Act. Personality is end-fulfillment; but an end-fulfillment which distills out of its very consummation the sacred substance of a universal activity—a cosmic symphony. The performers of this symphony are the seed-personalities who have achieved perfection through their own individual cycles, but, having thus achieved perfection, have consecrated it to a universal performance. The symphonic score is Man. Every fulfilled personality—every perfectly trained and masterful virtuoso in his own right—acquires immortality as one of the performers of the symphony, Man; and only thus. What he performs is a linear phase—a melody—of this symphony; and this is his spiritual reality, that into which he has "sacrificed," or rather consecrated, his gifts. His technique, his quality of tone and expression, his instrument remain, however, his own—to be recorded forever within the total performance.

How does this kind of orchestral participation differ from the organic participation of a leaf within a plant, of a tribesman within a tribal organism? It differs, first, in the fact that, while the leaf is born out of the plant with no choice of its own and no will or purpose of its own, the orchestra performer has come to the performance consciously and of his own volition, because he realized that through such a performance alone he would transform *a mortal consummation* into an *immortal participation*. The other basic difference is that all leaves are attached structurally, substantially and compulsively to stem and roots—all tribesmen are bound in their unconsciousness and instinctual nature to the tribe—while the participants in the symphony of Man are united only by their common will and aim; not substantially, but purposefully. They bind themselves—and they, even then, can fail in the performance and (until the Last Day) "drop out."

Leaf-participation is put in effect under root-compulsion, in unconscious structural unanimity; seed-participation is performed under qualified rules of action, deliberately accepted by the performer. In the latter, the only compulsion is that which resides in the integrity of the musical score to be performed; and this compulsion is *one with* individual purpose, because, the moment the performer freely assumes the responsibility of his participation in the performance, he accepts thereby the integrity of the score as the determining principle of his future activity.

Yet this seed-participation is more than the usual type of orchestral participation. It reaches deeper than a mere federation of wills for a common purpose, jointly decided upon. The symphonic score, Man, is not composed by the performers, and we are led to assume that the performance is directed by a guiding spiritual Intelligence. We may call the composer and the conductor, God. But if we do so, we must be careful to distinguish between the concept of a God Who is a Root-entity, a cosmic tribal and compelling Ancestor or Father—the God of all prae-Buddhistic religions —and the concept of a God Who is the symbolical Seed; from Whom the Father-God derives, as root derives from seed. It is from this Divine Seed that "man's common humanity" grew at the beginning of human evolution. And in the Last Day of this evolution, when the symphony of Man reaches the final stage of its performance in and through the all-synthesizing lives of personalities who have gathered to themselves all the harvest of eons of human civilization, then, Man will demonstrate fully his structural identity with the Divine Seed (or Logos) that was before Abraham (the Root) and *is,* now and until the end of the cycle. As this cyclic consummation takes place, a new Divine Seed will have been formed, not only in the likeness of the primordial one, but greater. For all truly integrated and consecrated personalities, throughout the human ages, will have contributed to the new Seed the spiritual character of their independent achievement of personality, the spiritual harvest of their most creative experience, their courage, their understanding and their nobility.

Personality ever creates divinity, while rooted in the common humanity of all men. As personality performs its melody in the immense symphony of Man, personality makes the potential, actual. What was in the beginning only "pattern" becomes "living tone" resounding through space. Intent becomes fulfillment; and fulfillment creates further goals and more inclusive purposes. And to him whose consciousness embraces beginning, development and completion, the dramatist, the performer and the performance are perceived likewise to be one—as seed, root and plant are one inclusive whole in essence and in consummated act.

Many a reader will no doubt label such concepts "mystical," and will seek by this simple device—especially if trained in "scientific" thought—to free himself from the trouble of pondering over the problems they pose and of facing the challenge of self-transformation which they imply. What an individualistic era, emphasizing unbridled "free enterprise" on the basis of traditional agriculture and small industry, is apt to consider as "mystical" and transcendental, a global society faced with the necessity of planning (at least within well-defined limits) and integrating its infinitely complex world-wide productivity may have to interpret as eminently practical—nay more, as a basic requirement for effective social functioning.

In closing the preceding chapter we indicated the undismissable need there was for the emergence of a new type of individual men and women able to fecundate with a new vision and a new purpose the confused and expectant masses of a humanity in a state of social, cultural and moral chaos. The appearance of such individuals implies however a reorientation of the most fundamental concept of personality; and this means necessarily a reorientation and revaluation of the relationship between man and society, between the purpose of individual existence and the purpose of society. This relationship, if it is to have any meaning at all, must have some kind of universal frame of reference—either a universe of blind and purposeless energies controlled by "laws" having arisen without any knowable reason or cause whatsoever, or a universe of spirit in which the infinitely varied types of activity which we discern are understood as expressions of divine purpose and ordering intelligence.

We consider it a practical and social as well as psychological necessity today to assume the validity of the latter concept. However, our concern here is not with the nature or transcendent character of divinity. We are not dealing with metaphysical issues *in themselves;* but only with the social imperative to transform and transfigure the ideal of personality, if humanity is to survive and meet creatively the new challenge of atomic power and of total productivity for all and by all. This "if" means very simply and practically that there must arise today and tomorrow a new type of creative individual persons, first, to conceive and to build the new "culture of plenitude," then, to operate effectively and harmoniously its "engines" and their controls for the maximum benefit of all men. The activity of such individuals must have a new quality. And it is *this quality of personal activity* which we have to define at all levels and in as many of its characteristics, implications and ramifications as is possible within the limits of a small volume.

This is therefore neither metaphysics nor mysticism. It is a matter of practical and demonstrable behavior. To enquire into the source and foundation of such a new quality of human behavior is necessary, if we are to understand this quality and to incorporate it consciously in our lives as individual persons. That such a new quality of individual behavior must imply a deep transfiguration of man's recent individualistic and quasi-anarchistic concept of personality and personal activity is the consequence of altogether new possibilities of social living. And it is the materialistic scientist who is responsible for these new possibilities, and not the so-called "mystic."

New powers demand new individuals and a new way of life. It is this new way which we must discover and define. Its application must of necessity transform profoundly the life of individuals and the pattern of society.

Harmonizing the Opposites
in the Lives of Individuals

THE TRANSPERSONAL WAY AND THE
NEW MANHOOD

When all the surface-tensions, side-issues and unessential conflicts which plague humanity today are sifted down; when man is willing to face in complete honesty and without emotional fear the essential evolutionary *need* of these times, one single fundamental problem clearly emerges, for us all to solve. It must be solved in individual lives; and it must be solved in the collective life of a humanity that has now been compelled, by one hundred years of technological development and by the devastation of total and global war, to recognize itself as a whole of interdependent parts and functions.

This problem is: *How to achieve steady and full productivity everywhere, through and for everyone, and at all levels of human activity, while providing for every human being the fullest, inalienable opportunity and incentive to live, act, think and feel as an individual person, in terms of consciously realized purpose, self-determined choice and creative responsibility to himself and to society.*

We have outlined the historical process within which the two factors of culture and civilization, of increase of seed and release of "fire," are constantly inter-related; and we have shown how human productivity, after long eras of scarcity, could be and had to become based upon the principle of global abundance (demonstrated in a "culture of plenitude") in order to cope with the requirements of atomic energy. We have discussed the concept of individual personality and its spiritual implications for men aware of their essential unity in terms of an all-embracing realization of creative purpose. It is on the basis of such a spiritual approach to personality that we can now formulate a way of reconciliation; that is, a type

53

of approach—personal and social—offering the possibility of resolving the virulent economic, social, political and ideological conflicts which are not only tearing down the fabric of our nearly obsolete Western culture, but (if unchecked) will lead to a complete breakdown of the civilization which at long last had made possible mastery over atomic energy.

A way of reconciliation. This means the ability to integrate the necessary respect for the freedom and creative development of the individual person, and the global organization of humanity along lines of total productivity. It means the ability to harmonize the opposite ideals of democratic individualism and of socialistic collectivism; individual freedom, and collective planning for total, permanent productivity; the right to choose one's personal vocation and rhythm of living through self-determination, and the need for an organic whole to control the functional behavior of its many parts in order to insure health and a balanced creative harmony in this whole.

A way of reconciliation is necessary; for should one of the opposing ideologies and social-political systems seek to impose its patterns over the other through war, there is little doubt that *both* systems would lose their present form and their constructive value; that, on the ruins of all nations a new primitive society would emerge, haunted by ghastly memories and compelled by psychological fear to begin again, from the deepest instinctual roots of mankind, a long evolution toward conscious intelligence and mastery over the energies of nature. A way of reconciliation is needed now; the pressure of historical forces leaves no other choice, and very little time. And it must be a positive, creative way; not merely a set of compromises which might succeed in avoiding for some time a head-on collision, at the cost of leaving man himself spiritually confused and emasculated. And it must begin in the individual person.

There can be only one way of integrating the aroused opposites, when these have crystallized into set systems and ideologies. It is to seek the solution of the dilemma *in man himself.* It is to establish anew the over-all and ultimate purpose of man; to define new goals and a new type of human being to achieve these goals. If two philosophies of life clash, a way of life must be sought which reorients both through new creative acts within a more inclusive frame of reference. If two types of minds cannot reach agreement on vital issues, then life must be made to flow more abundantly in both these minds; Man must speak more clearly through these minds —which means, that they must become more translucent to the spirit, the spirit which always answers all vital needs.

The principle of reconciliation is within man. To discover it requires the tapping of a deeper spring of the life of personality, as well as of the life of productivity. The individual must become reoriented to his work; the work must become reoriented to the individual. Personal integrity and maximum efficiency are not opposed within the individual life; they are not opposed within the global life of humanity. But humanity must realize its unity (as a person must realize his individuality and singleness of purpose) before men can learn to respect each other as individual persons within the framework of a completely efficient and productive global use of atomic energy.

When we speak of Man, with capital M, we refer to that indivisibility and singleness of purpose which it is now possible for every human being *concretely and effectively* to realize, to work for, to become consecrated to. The way of reconciliation is the way of a global purpose, which is Man. It is the conscious, rich, joyful, stirring, creative acceptation by every individual of this purpose. It is the acceptation, by each, of this purpose, Man, as an over-all and ultimate purpose. By such an acceptation, the individual establishes himself within a frame of reference that adds to his personality immense depth and takes nothing away from him but his fear and insecurity, his ghosts of scarcity and his prejudices. By such an acceptation, the individual makes his ego translucent to the spirit, his mind attuned to the harmony of that universal Intelligence which men call God. His whole personality becomes a ritual "mask" through which the purpose that is Man—"God's purpose"—is enunciated distinctly, with carrying power, with compelling sense; as much of this purpose as the individual is able to envision, to image forth, to understand, and to dare express.

The way of reconciliation is, therefore, the "transpersonal" way. It is a way according to which personality is made the servant of this super-personal all-human purpose. This purpose is not external to the individual person; if it were external we could speak of "mediumship" and not of a transpersonal life. The individual person *recognizes* this purpose as the meaning inherent in his own center, as the Word (*logos*) of which he is the incarnation. The individual transforms the center of personality into a lens to radiate outward that of which this center is, by inherent destiny, a distributive agency. And as this happens the personality becomes enhanced and filled with universalized potency and effectiveness: personality as a creative Source, as a power of evolution, as divinity-in-act.

What occurs then in the personality can be considered as a profound chemical repolarization of the very substance and magnetism of "human nature"—as we understand this term in our age of scarcity, of conflicts for survival, of fear and of greed. The personality becomes, as it were, "ionized". New powers are being liberated from it. "Man" is being released from the chrysalis of a particular man. Thereafter, the activities of this man become illumined and energized in a way; they acquire the character of inevitability, of answers to basic needs, of unchallengeable victory. The super-personal purpose, Man—or we might as well say "the Will of God"—acts directly through such an individual now advancing on the "transpersonal way". And in this sense we understand the words of the great French writer, St. Exupery, in *Flight to Arras* "The individual is a mere path, what matters is Man, who takes that path".

To say this is not, however, to reduce the significance and value of personality. The individual person remains the basic factor wherever human life and productivity express themselves in consciousness and in an individual sense of responsibility. The transpersonal life is not a denial of the ideals of personalism. It is a personal life *plus,* a personal life made receptive to the spirit, a personal life that is "transfigured"—yet first of all a life based on an integrated organism of personality. Before man enters upon the transpersonal way, there must be, *first* individualization and emergence from the womb of the tribe, the race, the taken-for-grantedness of communal living. There must be, *first,* consciousness out of the collective unconscious, a sense of individual responsibility assumed in "freedom". But consciousness, individual responsibility and so-called freedom, must not be considered as "things in themselves", or as objectives. They are to be realized instead *as powers to be used toward the fulfillment of a super-personal purpose.* The individual person is the user and "manager" of these powers; the super-personal purpose gives them direction and meaning.

The essence of individuality is purpose. It is purpose which individualizes; that is, which establishes a single, definite and distinct center around which the organic patterns of personality develop in effective integrated action. No man is truly an *individualized* person who is not permeated and dynamized through and through with a purpose—whether or not he is completely conscious of this purpose. With full consciousness of purpose, however, comes added effectiveness and concentration—and the deliberate discarding of the un-essential and the irrelevant. With full identification of individuality with purpose, the path is cleared for the inner realization of one's relationship to other individual persons equally consecrated to their essential purposes.

Then, purpose begins to be seen, not only as an individual factor, but as a *distinct mode of participation in the super-personal wholeness of Man*. The individual realizes himself as one in the midst of a creative Company, whose unity is understood as Man.

How could the individual man or woman be said, in any sense whatsoever, to be less for it? He certainly is no less a person. Personality does not shrink or lose its meaning and character by being flooded with transpersonal light potency; by being directed from within by a purpose whose roots reach to the very center of the universe. The transpersonal life is a personal life transfigured by an individual purpose that is established within the larger sphere of an inclusive, all-human or universal purpose. What the personality has lost is only its exclusivism, its spiritual "provincialism"—the weight of his prejudices and the psychological shadows that result inevitably from the very process of individualization out of a collective womb. What the individual person gains is the substance of his divinity: light, meaning, spiritual potency, immortal participation in Man.

He has gained all this by subordinating his pride and his re-oriented ancestral instincts to a central purpose; by integrating freedom and purpose, the many energies of human nature and the one power of a purpose established in the sphere of divine Harmony.

Freedom through purpose

The problem of freedom has taken a crucial importance in our world buffeted by the stormy conflict between democracies which uphold the theoretical freedom of the indivdual, and totalitarian societies which, in the name of the greater good of the people as a whole, curtail sharply this freedom of the individual. The word "freedom"—like the words "God" and "spirit"—can mean almost anything. The most that can be said intelligently of its use in all and sundry places is that it indicates a general *direction* or quality of behavior, rather than a specific and universally agreed upon goal to be reached once and for all.

To be free is, theoretically, to be able to act without outside hindrance. A free activity is an activity in which the individual feels no compulsion, save the decisions of his ego. As there are many basic types of human activities—such as thinking, working, talking, holding intercourse with other men, expressing one's opinions, etc.—so, men seek and fight for freedom of thought, freedom of work, freedom of speech, freedom of association, freedom of press. The freedom asked is the freedom of doing something in any way one wishes. And because this "doing" always involves other persons—and thus society as a whole and social patterns of behavior—the tendency is for the powers that rule society to interfere with this free activity by making it subservient to over-all regulations and compulsions. Certain types of freedom are thus denied. Certain types of activity must follow set social patterns or be conditioned by the compulsory allegiance to traditions, collective ideals and taken-for-granted goals.

In various countries it is assumed today as a matter of unchallengeable principle that the welfare of the whole is more important than the welfare of the part, and that therefore if the interest of the community as a whole requires that the tendency of individuals to act or express themselves in any special way be curbed, there is no end to which the community can go in compelling the individual; and this is shocking to the "free" citizens of democratic nations who hold that certain basic individual rights are absolute, sacred and inalienable. Nevertheless, our democratic freedom of action, even under the most "rugged" type of individualism, is greatly limited *by our standards of value.*

American millionaires are free to spend thousands of dollars giving an extravagant debutante ball next door to crowded slums and long lines of starving, freezing people waiting for a bowl of soup. But a man is not free to walk down public thoroughfares

without any clothes, or to move into an un-occupied house not belonging to him, even if there is no other place where he can sleep.
Can we not easily imagine a kind of society in which the former
type of activity would be far more outrageous to social standards
than the latter? What determines our conception of basic and necessary freedom for the individual is thus always our idea of what is
more valuable or less valuable for human beings. One type of
civilization believes that for every man to be free to produce for
society up to the maximum of his native potentiality is the most
essential individual freedom; another, that for every man to be
free to think and speak as he pleases is the greatest of all freedoms.
Any society will insist on guaranteeing what it believes is most
valuable, if necessary at the cost of what is thought to be of relatively secondary importance.

Of late, a new type of freedom has been publicized—freedom
from fear, freedom from want, freedom from all essential social
evils. Thus we have the positive freedoms *of,* and the negative freedoms *from.* We demand freedom "of " action, and freedom "from"
social evils. The one question, however, that is not usually asked is:
freedom *for what?* The one fact that is not brought forth is that
there may be no real significance in gaining freedom . . . for no purpose. Modern man should understand that his concept of freedom
has been in most cases a concept of rebellion, a negative concept.
Freedom has meant, in the historical past of the last two or three
centuries, freedom from the tyrannic power of church dogmas or
royal decrees—and today of a totalitarian State controlled by a
ruthless Party. Man has sought desperately freedom as a protest
against bondage—an emotional and intellectual protest.

Protest is a necessary phase; and so is the will to liberation,
whether it be political or spiritual. The emphasis upon creative
freedom and individual personality is necessary in as much as we
live in a de-personalized, mechanized, standardized society dominated by general patterns and regulations, red tape that stifles

personal initiative, and impersonal "scientific" laws which, *because they can only refer to statistical averages,* leave out of the mental picture the creative power inherent in the particular individual person.

It is necessary; but today it is not enough. Indeed, the exclusive emphasis upon the gaining of freedom by any one, under any condition—just like the indiscriminate application of the principle of national "self-determination" to any racial group who makes a claim on the evidence of past historical events—confuses rather than clarifies the real issue. What is essential today is not actually *how much* freedom human beings will obtain in their social or personal life—always a relative value—, but *to what purpose* this freedom will be put.

That this is so is demonstrated by the fact that today such destructive powers have been placed at the potential disposition of individuals or small groups, that the controls of these powers by the whole community of nations is absolutely indispensable. We do not refer here only to atomic energy, but also to the various possibilities which some individuals or groups have in modern society to dominate and to destroy the political and economic life of multitudes. And the same might be said in reference to psychic and mental, or religious values.

Freedom always means the freedom to use power. The greater and potentially more destructive the energies available, the more fateful for humanity the granting of freedom to those who have not established first of all their ability to use this freedom for a superpersonal beneficent purpose. Freedom is not a thing-in-itself, or an end in itself. Its value to the whole humanity—and obviously to the one who uses it—depends upon the purpose to which it is put. Even to have freedom and not to do anything with it is still a way of using it: a negative way—which in turn reacts, socially, as an encouragement to tyrannical or destructive abuses by others.

In most cases, the "free" person will use his "free" time by following aimlessly and with no particularly significant or individually directed intention various kinds of pastimes which are traditional, well advertised, fashionable, or which chance to attract his attention. He will therefore have gained freedom merely to see himself in bondage to social compulsions *against which he can not even rebel because he does not see them as compulsions.* He slides into the movies habit, the radio habit, the travelling habit, or more sophisticated and supposedly "cultured" habits. What has he gained, essentially and spiritually, by being free to do as he pleases? Very little else, often, beside the ability to waste his life and his time in activities which are unproductive, unrelated to the vital needs of human evolution, and spiritually meaningless—or worse!

The responsibility for determining a conscious purpose to freedom, a clear and significant purpose to the use of power and wealth, cannot be shirked. It cannot be shirked by any individual, no more than by any nation. The problem confronts everyone. It confronts every man who demands greater personal freedom or more "free time", every individual or nation who insists that freedom be given to other men who are less free.

Freedom is meaningless if considered as an absolute factor unrelated to our sense of participation into some group or community. Freedom cannot manifest as lack of relation to others, and make sense. Freedom, realistically and concretely understood, is the ability to "change gears". It is *the capacity for selecting, as an individual ego or an individual nation, the character, level and scope of the binding relationship one has to society, humanity or the universe.* To stay "out of gear" is not freedom. It is sheer inertia or self-destruction. It is, at best, merely postponing an inevitable choice. To be free is to be able to change, without external pressures or unjustifiable inner compulsions, one's type of allegiance.

"Allegiance"—a great and significant word! It means the character of one's *binding relationship* to some person, group or concrete ideal that incorporates or defines the purpose for which one claims individual freedom. Freedom without allegiance is purposeless freedom—and by allegiance we do not mean a verbal acknowledgement or a perfunctory sense of relationship. To give allegiance is to bind one's will in terms of a definite purpose, fully and consciously accepted. Where there is no binding, there is no steady relationship. Where there is no steady relationship, there is only anarchy. To be free is to be able to pass from a steady relationship, allegiance or purpose to another. But this process of change (i.e. freedom) can never be truly significant and constructive if the direction and purpose of the change are not conscious, clear, and fully acceptable to the individual. That it should be so is the essential point—rather than the manner in which the change occurs.

Freedom of choice does not mean the ability to make *any* choice. It is the ability to make a choice consistent with what one knows oneself to be; a purposeful and significant choice in terms of a purpose known, or deeply felt, to be valid. A youth who would be, theoretically and socially speaking, absolutely free to do whatever he wants can be considered the most un-free of all persons, if he has been given, or has reached by himself, no realization of *what his freedom is for*—that is, if having no positive sense of relatedness, he drifts along, compelled (without his knowing it) by circumstances and collective fashions. Indeed the worst bondage is to be bound by one's desire for purposeless freedom. It is bondage to a negative; bondage to the sensation of being "out of gear".

Every positive binding to a relationship, a group or a purpose has value, once it is accepted as a means to an end, as a phase of growth. Indeed, the basic difference of value is not between being bound and being free, but between the qualities and the purposes of the various possible types of "binding relationships"—i.e. of allegiances. And to come to realize this as a true fact is perhaps one of the most urgent and vital needs of the so-called "free" peoples of the world. What humanity questions today is not the degree of their freedom, but the vital character and validity of their allegiance; not how free they are, politically and otherwise, but what they are free for—which concretely and actually means: what they have bound themselves to.

Because an era is ending and a new one beginning, because the release of new and startling powers is compelling us all to revise our sense of value and to build new instrumentalities and new controls to manage these powers in our inner and outer lives, our century is witnessing a basic "change of gears" in human society. This means freedom, but it means even more new values, new purposes, a new allegiance to new gods and new ideals of relationship. Wherever men demand the freedom to make this new allegiance and to bind themselves to the destiny of a new humanity and a new civilization, to refuse them that freedom is to oppose evolution or the "will of God". And there can be no greater evil, no more monstrous crime against life. But whoever seeks freedom for aimless self-gratification, for paltry comforts, and above all just for the sake of "feeling free", has not yet learnt the meaning of true freedom.

Does this imply, then, that freedom should be denied to human beings groping toward the state of fully individualized personality, to confused and struggling individuals or groups, and to enslaved peoples; or that it should be restricted wherever, in so-called free nations, it is geared to no significant purpose? Indeed, *not*. Such a policy, whenever tried out—even perhaps with good intentions!— has always led to ruthless or subtle forms of oppression, by the state or by the church. Humanity is in a chaotic state of transition; but there is no way out of it *except forward*—forward to a *new* allegiance, clearly understood or deeply felt out of the impact of human experience upon individuals or groups who have been free to experience, to repudiate, and to adhere—in whatever way is possible to them—to new purposes.

The rational or individualized determination of new goals is not always possible. There are many ways of choosing, many ways of establishing new allegiances. What matters primarily is the *quality* of the allegiance, rather than how it was established. Faith is, in this, as necessary as reason, deep feeling as significant as intellectual judgment, intuition as valid as analytic reason. A community may make its allegiances as a whole; as well as individuals, as individuals. We have no right to impose upon any man or nation the *technique* by which it is to determine the purpose, or the character and scope, of this freedom.

What is our right and duty, however, is to *educate* ourselves, and others if need be, into the realization that freedom is not an absolute or an end in itself, but only a means to an end; for, like the "critical states" of matter, it is a phase of dynamic becoming between two modalities of being—two types of allegiance. That men should be able to use this phase of activity in order to pass from a lesser to a greater allegiance and purpose, they must know what this much-wanted freedom is for. Knowing what it is for, they may begin to find freedom in conditions where previously they could see only the absence of it; and they may discover bondage where before they glorified in the illusion of freedom!

This, then, is the reality of freedom: It is, for any human being, to express the one spiritual purpose of his individualized existence as a person, through activities which are necessary to that purpose— and only through these. Furthermore, as the worth of freedom is determined by the universal value, the living quality of meaning and the inclusiveness of the allegiance to establish which freedom was necessary, to be truly free, for any man conscious of the purpose of human existence, is to swear an irrevocable allegiance to Man. It is to accept no lesser purpose than that which derives from the place and function of humanity in the universe, from the powers which men, having released, must use. Men able to handle only puny powers can be allowed to work and to feel, to think and to plan in terms of puny purposes. But men who can tap the power that feeds the life of the sun have no other alternative than to become radiant with a purpose whose scope is as inclusive as the space to which the sun gives life and light—a divine purpose.

To live according to the transpersonal way is so to live that, *through* the concentrated fullness of focalized and consecrated personality, this divine purpose, in which the individual person finds his ultimate function and identity, is constantly being enacted by means of "necessary" acts, thoughts and feelings. Such "necessity" is the highest expression of creative freedom.

Man, the illumined "seed"

It is only on the basis of this sense of creative freedom which is also creative necessity that men, whose minds have become clear lenses to focus the transforming power of human evolution and divine purpose, can become moulders of tomorrow and seed of the new culture of plenitude. To such men belongs the inescapable duty to build the techniques and instrumentalities, the social institutions and the cultural forms which are to establish the controls for the necessary release of atomic power. These many structures which are needed, if this power is to be released constructively and harmoniously for *all* men to profit by, must be radically new— simply because the power they must control is also without parallel and precedent.

The change from the now becoming obsolete European culture to a new global civilization must without doubt be as complete as is spectacular the change from horse power to the atomic engines about to be built. It is not a matter of relatively superficial social transformation, such as that between the old Egyptian cities and the Rome of the Caesars, between the Phoenician fleet and the Roman or even medieval vessels venturing far away from the coasts. The difference in character, intensity and scope between the powers used in the century that saw the Declaration of Independence and those

about to be made universally available is basic, and appalling. It is
appalling simply because this change makes upon human beings,
individually and in a group, momentous and nearly unbearable
demands. It compels men to become almost at once transfigured
and renewed in a way that indeed taxes to the breaking point their
powers of imagination and of self-determination.

This is the crux of our present world-problem, far more than the
rivalry between Anglo-American individualism and Soviet Eurasia's
collectivism. This rivalry is part of the pattern of world-transfor-
mation for mankind; for it is, as we shall see presently, the expression of the inevitable polarization which must manifest in a
global organism—just as medieval France was divided (that is,
polarized) into complementary Northern and Southern cultures
and languages which finally became integrated after Joan of Arc's
martyrdom, on the basis of the still older Celtic foundation, into
the modern French nation. What way the global rivalry will develop is the great question which the decades ahead will have to
solve. But such a question can only be answered by human beings—
and in our present civilization mostly by, *both,* men who control in
a traditional way the social, political and economic mechanisms
of the national lives of all countries, and men who are able to fire
the imagination of the people with a new vision and a new faith.

The first group, save for a few exceptions, includes men whose
minds and feelings have been rigidly set into cultural moulds, and
who therefore must cling to old patterns and obsolete privileges
with a tenacity born of fear and insecurity. At best these leaders can
only be expected to "muddle through", along a course which will
avoid the worst cataclysms and will give time for the new and
creative voices to be heard widely. The real burden of creative
destiny belongs to these "voices" wherever located and from whatever strata of society they may arise. And this destiny can only be
fulfilled by men whose voices resound from a depth that reaches far
beyond their personal power of utterance, and whose words are

multifarious expressions of the Incarnate Word that is God's (or evolution's) purpose *at this time.*

By this, we do not mean necessarily that a new Christ-being is to appear who will reveal to mankind how to live in the Atomic Age. Many people expect such a divine Manifestation, and the Bahais believe that it has already occurred a century ago in Persia. What we mean is that, whether or not *one* human being becomes the most "central" focus for the descent of spirit which must inevitably answer the basic need of the times, *many* men must become "differentiated" foci for the social, cultural, economic and political manifestation of the spiritual impulse or *logos* which is to transfigure humanity. It may not matter too much whether or not the men who can summon the new images of man, woman and society are clearly conscious that they are "agents" for a release of spirit and that they serve what one may call either Man, or God's purpose. It is evident, however, that these men have always somehow to feel that theirs is a super-personal task, purpose or mission. Even atheist Lenin knew himself a man of destiny profoundly consecrated to the future of humanity. And because a medium-like Hitler who saw himself as God's voice is used by the destructive forces in humanity to serve the catabolic phase of evolution, it does not mean that other men cannot focus the constructive, anabolic processes of human growth while realizing that *through them* a divine purpose is given utterance.

This "through them" implies conscious determination, individual choice and vibrant realization of a super-personal purpose; not a passive type of quasi-mediumship. Personal passivity cannot go together with the state of being a creative agent for God's purpose or Man. Personal passivity and a disintegrated psychic condition devoid of any self-control can only lead to psychic and mental subservience, or slavery, to a destructive force. And all life is a field for the operation of, both, catabolic and anabolic processes.

The man who seeks to live the transpersonal life and to become an agent for the constructive and creative aspect of human evolution must, first of all, be a positive personality. He must be a radiant, convincing, stirring individual; a man who affirms and who loves, not one who denies and who hates; a man who includes as much as can organically and safely be included, not one who casts away whatever does not at once easily fit into preconceived patterns based on fear and personal frustration; a man who establishes a new approach and a new goal to meet the challenge of newly released powers, not one who revives an ancestral life-attitude as an expression of a psychological "return to the mother".

Such a man must be, symbolically, a "seed"—an illumined seed. He must incorporate in his integrated and solid personality the answer of human life to a need; and his must be a transforming and transfiguring answer to that need, for it is man's essential nature that it is always in need of transformation and renewal; for it is man's greatness that he can always be greater.

The need of humanity summons forth an answer from the spirit. This answer is a *logos;* a transforming "word", a transfiguring power. It is, both, an idea and the power to make this idea viable and alive among men. It is a "revelation" of the new purpose of human society and the "living Waters" which quench the spiritual thirst of men who had become barren souls and intellectual wastes. Every *logos* can thus be symbolized by an "illumined seed", because in the seed there is, latent, the structure of the future plant, and the life-energy necessary to impel the incorporation of ideal structure (archetype) into concrete organism.

A "seed-man" is a man whose creative vision focuses into eventual concrete manifestation a new social or cultural organism among men of his or (usually) the following generations; whose personality is sacrificed (i.e. spent in consecrated, transpersonal activity) so that a new type of human beings may live and, living, learn how to use constructively a new kind of power. There are men whose function it is to release this new kind of power; others are bent upon the task of imagining and projecting the new type of personality which will have the ability to manage and to use for the good of all this new power. Both categories of men are needed; but today as an abundance of unused or misused energies are weighing upon and endangering the future of humanity, the most urgent need is for men who may be exemplars and illumined seeds, whose spiritual progeny may be a new type of men and women.

In all such creative social and collective processes, polarity is always as basic a factor as it is in biological procreation. And the most obvious kind of polarization is that in which the "seed men" confront the common people and their need. There must be such a polarization, not in the futile and uncreative sense of a ruling aristocracy or intellectual elite which stand proudly aloof from the uncultured masses, but in the vital and vibrant sense of a true leadership fecundating the whole people with creative images, enlightening ideas and stirring goals. Today this polarization between creative individual personalities (who embody the masculine principle of *formative and spirit releasing mind*) and the people at large (who represent the feminine polarity of *life-energy and collective substance*) must take a form different from that it had in "cultural" periods; because now we are in the midst of a period in which "civilization" and its release of a new Fire are the dominant factors. Whether culture or civilization receive the strongest accent in any one century determines the essential psycho-mental character of the group of men who focus the creative social forces of the period.

During cultural epochs the intellectual elite constitutes itself a "feminine" pole, in as much as it is busy mostly with the production of cultural objects, of architectural edifices to house the various types of social or religious rituals establishing a significant and effective communal life, of institutions and intellectual records. The "masculine", spiritually fecundative polarity acts from within the bio-psychic organism of the collectivity; it is the Great Ancestor or the gods of mankind at the tribal stage—or, in the European Middle Ages, the Christ-*mythos* providing the faith, the basic images and the conceptual goals inspiring all social-cultural activities. The difference between the cultured elite and the masses is, thus, merely that existing between conscious and unconscious productivity. The elite works in a more or less illumined and pure state of consciousness; the masses cultivate the soil of the earth and the undifferentiated substance of their collective psyche according to the regulations and traditions provided for them by the elite.

When, on the other hand, the fiery force of civilization has challenged the relatively static values of a culture, crystallizing because its original spiritual *mythos* has lost most of its fecundative power and inspiring intensity, the situation becomes radically altered. The masses of the people lose their homogeneity and restlessly seek for a new spiritual fecundation, as a new type of minds arise in their midst stirring discontent and repudiating the ancient images of the communal bio-psychic life. These minds are the "shakers and movers" of history. They ask questions. They challenge. They destroy peace. They rush into passionate adventures, either in the quest for a transcendent God whose universality renders obsolete the cultural gods or the popular saints of the past; or in the search for gold—that which gives power over anything that one might wish, wares and human persons alike.

All these restless and adventurous men seek primarily to release power; whether it be by increasing the pulse of human interchange (commerce, travel, love uncontrolled by social tabus)—thus the metabolism of the collective organism of society—, or by piercing beyond the appearances of things, analyzing away the static solidity of matter, and violently sundering the boundaries of all things—nations, religions, personalities, and atoms alike. These great catabolists set the stage for a new age by releasing the very factors which, at the same time, destroy the old order and condition the birth of the future. First, their emphasis is upon analysis and destruction, later, when faced with the result of the destructive forces they set into motion, they are compelled by the pressure of impending catastrophe to turn their focus of attention to the building of controls for the physical and social powers they themselves let loose.

Controls, however, are useless without the proper individuals to operate them effectively and *for the good of the people at large.* As long as the officially ruling groups and organizations still hold tight to the privileges they derived from old and crystallized cultural-economic-political structures, they will seek to confuse the issues and to drug the people by playing to their sensuality, their inertia, their selfish craving for comfort and happiness at all cost— or even by giving them a false feeling that their voice is important and respected.

The true war, then, is that which pits the representatives of the old culture and those men whose destiny it is—and whose conscious purpose it should be—to become efficient carriers of the new spiritual and creative seed (the *logos* of the new age). The goal for these men is *not* to represent the best of the old culture or of any culture that ever was. It is *to fecundate the mind and the imagination of the common people with a new vision, a new purpose, a new logos.* This *only* can strike the passive, confused and at least superficially artificialized masses of humanity with divine fire. This *only* can make them see the glamour of freedom to no purpose, the poisonous self-indulgence and the devitalizing sentimentality in which they have waded with senseless delight, as devices forged by privileged groups to keep them in a state of spiritual unproductivity and inability to respond to the call of men of new vision.

The desperate need is for these men—these seed-men—to become so permeated by, so effulgent with the creative spirit, that "the people" will turn to them in devotion, in expectancy, in co-creative partnership . . . yes, as woman, consciously facing her destiny and function rather than merely submitting to the compulsion of unconscious instinct, turns to the man who can fecundate her spiritually and "in-spirit" her with a new purpose.

Fecundative men—and the people. The people, as a feminine pole, must be weaned away from spiritual infantilism and skin-deep sensualism—and as well from the intellectualisms of our modern mentality. The people must be aroused into a most vibrant expectancy of spiritual seed. This seed, no individual as a mere individual, can give to the people. This seed is the mark of divine Sonship. Only those can bestow it upon humanity who are *avatars* of Man, focal points for the release of creative spirit, illumined persons. The way to this state of illumined and infinitely potent seed-hood is the "transpersonal way".

That there should be a new type of human beings, in order to resolve through actual living and creating the basic dilemma of our age opposing the freedom of personality to the requirement of total productivity for all and by all, means that there must be new ideals of manhood and womanhood. In the abstract, we can speak of the individual person without reference to sex. Actually the process of individualization must unfold in two distinct rhythms according as the personality reaching the status of individual—that is, of indivisibleness, singleness of purpose and conscious selfhood—nucleates around a masculine or feminine polarity.

Personality can be defined as *an organized human whole through which power is released into acts toward the fulfillment of purpose.* Personality, therefore, is basically conditioned toward the fulfillment of an individual purpose—or of a universal purpose—by the polar character of the power that energizes it. Here again the natural rhythm of the power to be used establishes the foundation of the mechanisms of use. These mechanisms in a human person are psycho-mental as well as physiological. As the purpose of any individual person *must be single if it is to be fully effective,* the whole personality (body, psyche, mind) must be structured as a unit by the polar rhythm of the power it is able to use. The basic type of productivity it can demonstrate most successfully is also depending upon the polarity (masculine or feminine) of the available power.

In the culture of plenitude, as complete a fullness of being and productivity as is possible will be demanded of every man and woman. Thus man and woman will need to operate with the maximum efficiency of their respective manhood and womanhood. But this does not mean what might be commonly or traditionally understood by such a statement! Simply because the ordinary age-old attitude toward manhood and womanhood is based upon *the unconscious performance of instinctive acts,* while the new attitude of a mature humanity composed of men and women who have reached a relative degree of fulfillment as individual personalities must center around *the conscious performance of an individually chosen purpose.*

This distinction is fundamental, even though it cannot be considered as absolute in most cases. It is a difference of direction, of basic rhythm—and once more of "quality" of power, or level of "fire." Biological power is primarily unconscious power; though it can become conscious and controlled effectively and usefully under certain conditions—as for instance in *yoga* and in scientific cultivation of seed. Atomic power, on the other hand, can only be handled consciously; and likewise the power of that creative mind which projects most effectively ideas as spiritual seeds. The new manhood and womanhood must therefore, in order to serve their fullest purpose in the culture of plenitude, operate in terms of conscious productivity. And there can be no fullness of productivity where this productivity is not geared to a purpose which is inclusive and universal: an all-human purpose.

It is only as this all-human purpose—which is Man—operates through the individual person who has consciously and freely identified himself or herself with one of its particular aspects, that freedom and necessity become reconciled, that the fullest productivity can be attained by a group of personalities consecrated utterly to the purpose of the whole. This is the transpersonal way; the illumined way. And it is the creative and conscious way which must supersede the unconscious way of procreative instinct, in whomsoever seeks to act as a seed-man, to participate in Man in terms of seed-participation—in contradistinction to leaf-participation, as we defined these terms.

In these critical years that may see the greatest victory humanity has ever won over the pressure of universal inertia and nature's entropy, the one great ideal of manhood can only be determined by this character of conscious and free participation. Creative men that are spiritually illumined seed, creative men that can stir the people of the world into the birth of a new culture of plenitude, creative men that are conscious agents through whom Man operates toward the fulfillment of divine purpose — these are the men the need of our tragic, but potentially glorious, century requires. Theirs is not to dominate with the brute male-hood of dictators and tyrants the people they drugged or cajoled into unconscious passivity. Theirs it is to "in-spirit," to fecundate with ideas, to arouse with a vision, to stir with the release of that Pentecostal power which is the fire of understanding and of truth.

There are such men. They must act *now*. Upon their united energy, their faith, their consecration and their skill, the destiny of our race depends.

TOWARD A NEW IMAGE OF WOMANHOOD

As there is a desperate need today for creative men able to fecundate the mind and the imagination of humanity with a new vision and a new purpose in order to meet the challenge of the release of nuclear atomic power and of the Age of plenitude which must come, so also there is a vital need for a new type of women who can act, feel and think in polar relationship to these men. For over a century women, the world over, have been stirred by intense restlessness and an often aggressive eagerness for liberation from the prejudices and the fetters which have characterized their social status for the past centuries or millennia. This crusade for woman's freedom has paralleled the rise of men who have worked deliberately, if often confusedly or blindly, with the "fiery force of civilization" challenging the value of the crystallized tyrannical structures of a society based on scarcity and privilege for the few.

We spoke of these men as "catabolists" who at the same time destroyed the obsolete culture of the past and released the power by using which the new age of total productivity, for all, in all and by all can now be ushered in. The same could be said of women who, in their attempt to re-polarize their way of life and to develop new powers of mind and conscious self-determination, have sought to transcend, and perhaps succeeded in transforming, some of the basic features of their natural character as women, while releasing new capacities oriented toward new spiritual goals. In its evolution from the thesis of unconscious bio-psychic instinct to the synthesis of conscious ideo-spiritual productivity on the basis of the fully mature personality, humanity has to pass through the antithesis of anarchistic and rebellious individualism—or through a nature-denying phase of transcendent idealism and ascetic non-productivity.

77

This evolutionary rhythm can be traced in every large-scale historical happening; indeed, no one can hope to understand fully any significant phase of collective human development if this basic rhythm is not taken as a broad frame of reference. The feminist movement is no exception. It has a deep relation to the world-crisis of our times and the future emergence of a society demonstrating the principle of productivity at a new level. It is an expression of the break-down of a period of relatively static culture and of the recent emphasis on civilization and its release of new human powers as well as of new cosmic energies. But it is also a phase of the still broader pattern of growth of humanity from the state of bio-psychic unconscious instinct to that of conscious and individualized mentality.

The situation of woman, collectively speaking, in the twentieth century world is affected by these various evolutionary and historical factors. Thus the complexity of the problem it poses. Here again a dilemma confronts us as we seek to reorient society and its basic forms of human relationship toward the new goals outlining themselves on the horizon of the Age of plenitude. This dilemma is a phase of the general one in which the need for respecting the integrity and freedom of the conscious individual person stands in contrast with the need for establishing patterns for total global human productivity at all levels. In relation to woman the two poles of the dilemma can be defined as: the right for any woman to be a consciously self-determined individual person, and the necessity for women to participate, with the fullness of their being, in the total productivity of the new society.

Woman's problem can be discussed within two frames of reference: in relation to society at large and to the general ideal of womanhood held by a particular culture or historical period—then in relation to the love which unites her productively, or regeneratively, to a man, and to her children or to her work. In the first case, we have to speak of woman in a collective sense; in the second case, the focus of our attention must be the relationship of woman to man and man to woman—its character, its purpose, and the nature of the love which alone can make it fully significant. In this chapter we shall limit ourselves to the first approach; and we shall seek to understand the meaning of the historical process according to which the ideal of womanhood has acquired its prevalent characteristics in modern society, especially in the Western world. On the basis of such an understanding we can then proceed to outline a new image of woman adequate to meet the exigencies of the challenges of the new era which is upon us.

The evolution of the Woman Ideal

The yesterdays of evolution and history are nearly always factors of bondage. They show what we must emerge from, the inertial pull of habits one should counteract at all levels, the taken-forgranted tradition which has to be deliberately challenged, the immediate cause of our frustrations and our socially conditioned failures. But the day-before-yesterday has usually much to offer to those striving toward new tomorrows—as thesis, in repolarized form, has much to offer to synthesis—provided we do not go to the extreme of worshipping the ancient roots, and of projecting our ideal of tomorrow upon this distant past, thus making it glow with an unearthly light.

The light of the ancient ages is, indeed, completely earthly; but it is earthly *in a spiritualistic, and not in a materialistic sense!* Man, then, is utterly bound by the earth; but the earth, to him, is spirit. Biological functions (such as sexual procreation) appear, to the man of the great tribal era, spiritual. Indeed, they *are* spiritual for him, because the creative power of human evolution, during this period is focused upon the processes of bio-psychic production. It is focused upon the evolution of a definite type of instrumentalities or organs necessary for the development of soil-cultivation and human culture. And this development proceeds according to the particular requirements of the several kinds of soil or climate, as well as of the several racial types, then in existence.

Tribal man, however, operates in unconsciousness as far as the normal individual men and women are concerned. Consciousness is collective (instinctive) and involved in rituals (socially and organically determined acts). Personality is tribal not individual. Productivity resides only in the tribe and the tribally significant relationship. Likewise ownership of land and of most instruments of production is communal—the use of these productive assets being ceremonially regulated and inherently "sacred." Indeed, everything truly productive and magically efficacious *in guaranteeing productivity* is sacred, by definition—only, in recent times, men have substituted the terms "religious" or "psychological" for the much misunderstood ancient word, "magical."

Biological productivity means production of seed and the increase of seed through the careful supervision and performance of all the natural operations connected with the seasonal processes of organic growth and multiplication. This is true of soil-cultivation, of cattle raising, of the production of tools and magical instruments (the original stem from which all artistic products, from jewels to modern symphonies, have branched out)—and it is true as well of providing the tribe with an increasing (or, at times, a regulated) number of children. The man-woman relationship—marriage and family—has significance, therefore, basically if not exclusively, in terms of the production of a necessary progeny *to the tribe as a whole.* The children are born to the tribe, belong spiritually to the tribe. The sexual union of man and woman has to be consecrated by the medicine man of the tribe and dedicated to tribal productivity. In many places this consecration takes the form of an actual ceremony in which the medicine man performs the sexual initiation of the virgin bride in the name of the tribal god, stamping her as it were with the creative personality of the god, in the name of whom he alone has the right and ability to act.

At this tribal stage, spiritual and creative potency is regarded as collective and as a divine bestowal. But when the men of the extended tribal society become more individualized and endowed with the increasingly definite spiritual character of personality, they become more and more masters in their own houses. The patriarchal family supersedes the tribal clan. The union of bride and bridegroom becomes of social, rather than tribal importance. It has nevertheless to be consecrated or blessed by a priest "in the name of God" in order to acquire a *spiritual sanction*.

As we come to the Christian era we find the concept of earthly tribal organism replaced by that of the Mystical Body of Christ— the universal (i.e. Catholic) Church, and ultimately the whole humanity. Tribal values, which had degenerated through centuries of individualistic emphasis, become revived, but at a transcendent level and within the universal and ideal (but not actual) framework of the "brotherhood of man." Biological cultural productivity is made subservient, as a spiritual value, to soul-productivity. Seed is considered merely as the means for manifestation of soul. Increase in seed has value only in so far as it serves the purpose of an increase of souls consecrated to a transcendent God. Such a consecration requires a prior process of purification and redemption —a transcending of human nature and of all that, in it, seeks productivity and increase for any purpose except that of glorifying God and augmenting the vitality and spread of the Mystical Body, the Church.

Thus, the central and recurrent theme of Christianity is redemption (spiritual transformation) rather than productivity. Because God alone can produce souls, and souls alone have ultimate value, man's essential duty is to liberate himself from his tribal earth-conditioned nature. Indeed he reaches his greatest value by sacrificing his bio-cultural productivity, and entering the state of asceticism or monasticism; therefore, by successfully transforming his natural capacity to produce into the ability to save, to redeem and regenerate himself—and to help others to do likewise. The Christian ideal is that of the Savior and the Saint—not that of the Producer; the goal is one of transcendence, not of fulfillment—overcoming of life, not abundance of life. Even outside of the orthodox religious field, European culture can be characterized by the symbolic figure of the Alchemist, who transmutes natural elements through fire. Even its empire-builders and conquerors have to cover their basic urges under the cloak of the desire to convert infidels to Christianity—to save souls.

Such an attitude changes profoundly the status of the Christian woman. Woman, who had been worshipped in ancient tribal religions as the great producer of organisms, and whose function had been seen on the background of soil-fertility and breeding processes, finds herself relegated to a plane of secondary value—just because she is the obvious symbol of biological productivity. And when the early medieval thinkers wonder whether or not women have souls—and also war against the arts and culture in general—they are simply translating in narrow and emotional terms the state of devaluation into which bio-cultural productivity has fallen since the origin of Christianity—and, to a lesser extent, since Plato and the Hindu transcendentalists and *yogis.* The mother of Christ, alone, is singled out (rather awkwardly, in view of the fact that Jesus had several brothers!), and miraculously considered as freed from the taint of biological productivity.

This mythos of the "Immaculate Conception" becomes in time the seed from which develops, during the great period of medieval culture (1000 to 1350 A.D.), a new image of woman. This transcendent image (which is to acquire a new and generalized meaning during the Romantic era) is formed in the minds and souls of medieval men under the influence of the profound psychological and intellectual changes occurring after the crisis of the year 1000 (when the "end of the world" is generally expected). It grows in influence during the Crusades, which bring the still semi-barbaric aristocracies of the West in contact with the Byzantine, Syrian and Arabic cultures.

The great spiritual movement designated by the name "Chivalry" serves as a focus to coordinate and direct this profound transformation of the medieval mentality. To it can be attributed the genesis of the two powerful images, the Knight and the Madonna ideal, which give a new meaning to human relationship and to social behavior—at least at the aristocratic-cultural level. Chivalry takes the basic and unavoidable state of feudal warfare as a foundation, and upon it builds spiritually significant themes. One kind of war and one type of warrior becomes consecrated, as "holy" expression of the "Will of God." The Crusade is preached as *transcendent war* waged in countries far and beyond the narrow confines of the lands of the West; the Knight, a transcendent warrior, who has "taken the Cross"—thus assuming vicariously the personality of Christ. His war against the Infidels is raised to the symbolic meaning of the universal struggle of spiritual man against his "lower nature."

The Madonna, on the other hand, is the transcendent mother, the sinless mother of Christ-like souls, the mother whose biological productivity is transfigured and redeemed by the divinity of the child she bore. Mary "conceived without sin"—and, at the psychological-cultural level we see the religious artist or philosopher also "conceiving" his cultural progeny without the sin of the separative intellect or the self-will, if his mind becomes as a pure vessel inspired (or in-spirited) by the Holy Spirit of Truth—by the Revelation of Christ.

The Madonna-image being applied to womanhood as a whole, woman becomes, as a result, the "redeemer through love," the intercessor or mediatrix between sinful, proud men and God. Dante crystallizes this transcendent ideal of womanhood in the person of Beatrice—she who leads man heavenward through the magic of "pure love." This is the Christian woman in her highest function, and the cult of the Virgin Mary that spreads fervently through the Gothic Ages resounds throughout the European centuries, at times overshadowing even the worship of the Christ.

As the Classical Period begins, and the strongly centralized government of Kings "by divine right" brings to a rigid focus the collective personalities of nations, the transcendent images created by the Age of Chivalry fade away. Individualistic men and intellectual women fill the turbulent stage of European history. The court-life absorbs the nation's creative energies and makes of woman a courtisane—in every sense of the word. Through her beauty or her wit, she acts as a certification of aristocratic rank and prestige to her husband. Her life fills with political intrigues or social contests. Indeed the spiritual changes into the political; and woman moves from the altar to the "salon"—neither transcendent in the medieval sense, nor productive in the tribal sense. She has children, by the way and as an unpleasant concession to nature; until birth-control spreads over an atomistic society whose petty greeds and conflicts are undertoned by the "war of the sexes." Woman, increasingly resenting her feminity, turns suffragette—and perhaps Lesbian.

Romanticism, however, in its desperate and often unbalanced attempt to counteract the intellectual dryness and the abstract rationalism of the Classical period, eagerly drinks at the source of medieval spirituality. The legends of the Gothic Age revived, the transcendent ideal of womanhood once more fires the imagination of poets and artists. The "redeeming woman" is enshrined in the disturbed soul of the Romantics. Redemption through love — whether of the intellectual and selfish man, or of the prostitute— sings as a leit-motive through the great cultural achievements of the nineteenth century; while the typically bourgeois society of the Victorian era prolongs the classical tradition of social intrigues and lust for power in a world where barons of finance and industry vie with old-time aristocrats.

In the United States of America, the woman Ideal evolves in a somewhat different manner. In the Southern States the place of the cultured woman is very similar to that she occupies in the English aristocracy or great bourgeoisie. In New England, or wherever the struggle against climate and nature is particularly hard and no slave labor available, the American woman displays a remarkable strength of character and hardihood, assuming a large share of the struggle for physical productivity. The opening of frontier lands makes increasing demands upon the woman; for the opportunities for physical conquest and economic enrichment being so great, and so overwhelmingly occupying the attention of rough and ready men, the women-pioneers find themselves entrusted with everything outside of clearing the soil and money-making—particularly with all educational and cultural activities.

This is something new in the world. In Europe, education has been almost everywhere in hands of the clergy, of monks or of male scholars. Only the privileged few were usually considered worthy of education, and the men who taught them, even when entirely separated from any religious authority, constituted a class with high standing in the community. Education had still kept something of its sacred origins, and it was aristocratic in character. Above all, it belonged to the men, who alone were in control of mental values.

In America, however, under the spur of a democratic ideology, of an expansion of printing and of the rapid spread of machine-power and technology, education becomes democratic and popular. Millions seek to learn what soon proves essential for financial success; for, the more complex the industrial background of society, the more involved its laws and its techniques. When the Civil War destroys the aristocratic culture of the South and gives an added opportunistic character to the more democratic and industrial North, when the westward exodus reaches definitely the Pacific Coast and the quest for gold makes of many men adventurers and what is politely called "rugged individualists," the peculiar features of

American education and American society become even more accentuated.

Women, as a result, assume a position of spiritual authority in
the family, and of cultural management in the community. They
control not only the production, but the spiritual-mental education
of children. The world of man and the world of woman drift apart.
Men are relegated to the economic sphere and to politics. At the
conscious, non-biological level, their function is almost exclusively
to make money, to produce and increase social power. In all other
ways, women establish themselves in a position of spiritual and
cultural superiority. As this occurs, the United States become increasingly a hot-house for "mother complexes," for "mother's boys"
and thus for men with a sense of spiritual-cultural inferiority —
which in turn compels them to concentrate further on being "bread-
winners," and little else. New images of man and woman take
shape in the subconscious of the race—"Mom" and "Dad"—; images which differ greatly from those developed by European culture.

Are they constructive and spiritually fruitful human ideals? Most
likely they are not. They are indeed the products of a peculiarly
stressful period in American history; a period highly successful, ma-
terially, but none too fortunate, spiritually. It is the period conditioned by the tragic aftermaths of the Civil War, the Spanish War,
World War I (and we have probably to say, World War II); a
period during which battles have been won, but peace has led to
spiritual defeatism and a loss of moral values. Post-war failures
have resulted from national immaturity, from isolationism, from
the lack of understanding of social and international responsibility,
from concentration on material problems—and also, in this century, from a wholesale psychological instability. The "Mom" image
has no doubt been at least partly responsible for much of this instability in men who were so eager "to go home"—to homes which
nevertheless had very little to offer them in the way of creative in-

centives and of spiritual stimulation, the most necessary virtues at the threshold of the atomic Age and of an entirely new global society.

A new image of woman is indeed one of the most basic needs of American society, and as well of the democratic society of western Europe. And in determining its essential characteristics we should never lose sight of the long evolutionary process which, underneath the relatively superficial tensions and problems generated by the Industrial Revolution and the breakdown of European culture, has brought to woman a deep and far-reaching challenge of repolarization at a new level of spiritual awareness and of response to the creative forces of the universe. The transcendent image of woman, whether medieval or romantic, was the expression of an unresolved conflict between biological nature and the Christian idea of Soul; between instinct and spirituality. The new image will have to be one, in which and through which this conflict is resolved.

Feminism did not, and could not, produce of itself such a conflict-resolving image of woman, because it was not directed toward fulfillment, but rather toward liberation from bondage. It released energy but did not provide a basically new image of integration for woman, or for society as a whole. Feminism gave woman the collective incentive necessary to overcome her social-economic limitations; but it should be regarded even more as an attempt by woman to transcend—consciously, deliberately, and collectively—the biological and emotional compulsions of her nature, and to emerge with a personality focused at the level of the intellectual and abstract mind.

This effort was spurred on in America by the fact that men, collectively speaking, had accepted a position of spiritual-mental inferiority; that fathers were far too often unable to appear as symbols of inner authority to their daughters (because of the mother's patronizing and superior attitude); and that the majority of husbands did not actually fill the psychological (or sexual) needs of their wives—whether or not the latter were conscious of the fact. Such a state of affairs, frequent in American families, has produced what Jung's psychology calls the *animus* type of woman, a type in which intellectual pride and social ambition, a critical mind and a worship of official opinions or methods, develop as psychological substitutes for a deeply satisfying relationship with father or husband.

Such a type of woman seeks to transcend her biological compulsions by developing a masculine "persona"—an official and over-conscious, over-deliberate attitude of intellectual (or "occult") importance. But this brings her neither peace nor fulfillment in real personality. She does not succeed, except in the rarest instances, to reach the mystical transfiguration or the idealistic quietude of the medieval nun, who also sought to overcome the biological pull of her nature. She is the creature of an age of intellectual criticism and emotional restlessness, an age that repudiates the religious-mystical type of transcendence of the Catholic and universalistic Middle Ages, but has yet found no "image of salvation," no new "principle of integration" which alone would give to humanity a new and more inclusive sense of fulfillment and productivity. And woman, even more than man, finds it very hard to resist the sway of collective belief and collective patterns.

Woman's problem today is the problem of the whole Christian civilization. Liberation, mystical redemption, scientific progress, technological discoveries are all phases in a wholesale process of transition from unconscious instinct and biological tribalism to Platonic rationalism and intellectual freedom. But the very concept of "overcoming nature" and of "reaching beyond" (transcendence) is by definition a concept of transition or repolarization. This concept introduces necessarily psychological conflict wherever it becomes a living ideal—unless the transcendental goal, and the person's devotion to someone who has attained it, overwhelm almost entirely the attitudes, instincts and behavior to be transcended.

Whether or not she is conscious of the fact, woman is caught more deeply in the web of biological compulsions or preoccupations than man. The biological rhythm of fertility is impressed regularly upon her mind and it affects her whole behavior. If women succeeded in forgetting these compulsions generally, there would be no more children and no more humanity. Thus the modern woman has found herself in the basically unsound position of having to center her attention constantly in two opposite directions; of having to overcome and transcend something she could not *collectively* overcome or transcend. In her, intellectual activity is pitted against natural instinct; and spirit is made to be the antagonist of a resented nature.

Man can stand better such an interior conflict of consciousness, because his sexual nature is characterized by positive and fecundative action—and spirit and creative thought also operate in a positive and fecundative manner. His problem is thus essentially to learn to act in a similar positive way at two levels instead of one; then, of transferring the essential focus of his attention, his desires and his personality from the biological to the spiritual-mental level. But woman's dilemma is far more critical, and her conflicts are far more devastating, because in many cases, subconsciously if not deliberately, she tries to be receptive biologically and somehow to act as a positive fecundative masculine mind at the social-intellectual level.

These conflicts are so tragic that woman would never be led, and able, actually to open her nature to their nearly insoluble problems unless she were psychologically or biologically frustrated by the failure of her men—father, lover or husband—, and, in a still broader sense, by the spiritual failure of the civilization to which she contributes her progeny. The medieval nun was able to solve her conflicts because she did not try to oppose spirit or mind to nature. She, instead, sought to demonstrate her woman nature at a transcendent, mystical level. She retained, fully and uncomprom-

isingly, without evasion, subterfuge, or resentment, her woman nature. A transcendent Christ, and not a physical man, became her
lover and fecundator. And His love and fecundation was indeed
real and poignant to her; it had to be, if she was to attain peace,
radiance and spiritual fulfillment.

Woman's goal in our modern world can be, only in the rarest
cases, such a transcendental state of polarization and integration by
a mystical Image. But neither should woman's goal be a protest
against her nature and the productive rhythm of her nature. What
woman can do is to express her nature, or better still, her natural
character, at two levels—at the biological and at the psycho-mental levels. What the new woman must indeed achieve is an integration of these two aspects of her nature around a spiritual center
operative in both realms and giving spiritual meaning to both
types of activity. And this integration will be productive, because it
will be true to life and evolutionary purpose. Woman's productivity
will cease to be unconscious and compulsive. It will become conscious and planned, geared to abundance and total fulfillment, spiritually illumined. And this productivity will become fully and
harmoniously integrated with man's productivity—as culture will
be integrated with civilization, and the process of increase of Seed
with the release of the universal Fire. New values will thus be
created by harmonious men and women, and a new humanity in
whom spirit will act in an ever renewed epiphany.

Woman in the fullness of her nature

We have to define "woman's nature," if the above statements
are to make sense; and our definition must be such as to be as valid
at the psychological as at the biological level.

The natural character of woman is to incorporate, at all levels
of consciousness and behavior, the expectation of the present for
the future, of today for tomorrow. It is to be the "cup" ready to
receive the creative stir and the new logos of the spirit—be this sym-

bolic cup a womb or a Grail. In this sense, woman's natural character is to be the eternal virgin in expectation of creative tomorrows. And this is the true symbolical meaning of the Immaculate Conception: to "conceive without sin" is to bear progeny without losing this vibrant quality of expectancy, this power to summon ever more radiant creative acts from man or from God. The spiritual sin of woman is to settle within what she has, to be satisfied with yesterday's impregnation and today's harvest, to cease expecting new miracles. The earth's nature always expects a new spring. It is never tired of bearing seeds that will grow into a new vegetation. It never ceases to demand of the sky and the sun new dawns, more flamboyant sunsets. It has always more gold to give to the trees for their autumnal apotheosis.

Woman's expectancy should operate at all levels—that is, at all the levels at which a masculine, fecundative power can give a vital and life-giving answer. It is her expectancy which summons this positive, spirit-releasing or fire-releasing, power to a new outpouring. In this expectancy the entire *past* of the world and of the human race comes to the chalice stage of a *present* calling forth into its cup the creative logos or vision that is the *potential future*. Woman's natural character and function is to give substance to the need of life and humanity; but, further still, it is to transfigure this need with the expectation of its fulfillment. To need a new outpouring of life or spirit is not enough. To need a new and greater harvest, or salvation from sins of inertia and failure, is not enough. The need must be infused throughout with the expectancy of God's —or man's—creative answer. And this is what prayer means: a need pervaded and set aflame by expectancy—a demand made in utter faith that it will be answered.

Life and spiritual growth proceed ever onward from expectation to fecundation, then to fulfillment. But in the heart of every fulfillment, there must sound the mysterious small voice of a new and deeper need, which, eventually growing into an intense and poignant expectation, once more calls forth a new fecundation. Woman fulfills her natural character and plays her part in the birth of cultures by expecting man to release the power and the new seed which will make manifest the next step in cosmic and spiritual evolution. *As her expectancy is, so will be the creative answer.* Hers may not be the creative vision, but hers is the conditioning of that vision; for spirit never acts except in answer to a need poignant enough to call forth an answer. Neither does man create except in answer to the need of a woman-element, either within his own psyche, or in his community, or in the body and soul of the beloved.

But if—out of fear, pride or spiritual inertia—the woman (or the community) refuses to recognize and admit the need, and to transform it into a powerfully shaped or consciously formulated expectancy, then she closes herself to the outpouring of spirit; and she can only fill her inner life with mental reflections and devotional illusions. She can only draw to her soul the glamour of intellectual phrases or of "psychic" images, the spiritual dizziness of a world of transcendent fantasies and emotional lies. Such is the case of the modern intellectual woman, whose father-complex leads her to a stereotyped subservience to, and emulation of, academic intellectual attitudes, and "authorities" in learning. Such also is the case of the modern "occultish" or devotional woman flitting from Hindu *swami* to the Western hierophants of resurrected Mysteries.

In both cases, the woman fails fundamentally to accept, and to act according to her natural character. She is not satisfied to condition the creative future by bringing to a clear focus and formulation the need of her race or community, and by intensifying her radiant faith and expectation to a pitch which must of necessity draw to her the in-spiriting personality that will make her fecund, a mother of the world of tomorrow. And she is not satisfied with this, either because her adolescence has been frustrated by an inadequate father and a possessive mother, or because, in her pride or

her fear, she would rather worship and be priestess of some officially respected or mysterious idol, than become empty as a chalice
that the yet un-known God or man will have to fill with the living
waters of futurity.

Woman's magic is in her emptiness. It is the magic of *Tao,*
which means not only "the Way", but also is to be interpreted as
that to whose inner void all things are drawn, and from which all
lives are reborn, aglow with dawns. It is true that many a woman
instinctively knows this; but knowing it, she often uses her indraw-
ing power to capture, possess and absorb the releaser of spirit, or
the man still haunted in his psychic depth by a compelling mother-
image. She is then the "possessive mother" or the "dark woman"—
or even the "redeeming woman" who, the Romantic French writer
A. Dumas Jr. once said, "inspires in us great things, which she,
then, proceeds to make impossible for us to accomplish." As this
occurs, she claims increasingly *for herself* as an individual the power
she has fixed—and apologizes for the powerlessness of him whom
she has made captive to her psychic positiveness and her glamour,
whether or not she is aware of the fact and of her purpose. The
magic of expectancy is gone. Man is made a provider to standardized demands and meaningless hungers. When sex and love become
a hunger, they cease to be creative and spiritual. They fill today
with ghosts of yesterday, not with the potential of tomorrow.

Productivity is the fulfillment of life's needs—or of social-psy-
chological needs. And productivity, in the realm of culture, is based
on expectancy; for without the expectation of spring and of new
life, no human being would have ever toiled to plant seed in a soil
previously made "empty." The realm of culture is essentially woman's
realm; but culture is born of the impact of the new creative powers
released by civilization which is man's essential domain. Man releases the physical or spiritual Fire; woman feeds and multiplies the
seed. She builds organisms or mechanisms for the controlled use
of Fire.

Both operations can be unconscious and instinctual, or conscious and directed by lucid intelligence and the perception of goals and meanings. In the tribal stage of society they were unconscious. Under the impetus of transcendental philosophies and religions, since the prae-Buddhistic period of India's Forest-Philosophers and of the earliest Upanishads, biological instinct has been transformed into intellectual consciousness, and dim feelings into clearer psychological responses to social and spiritual challenges. This process of transformation has been strenuous; it has accentuated inner conflicts, religious emotionalism and political warfare—and it is far from completed. Nevertheless, the time has come when, *as far as the collective life of humanity is concerned,* the emphasis upon the scientific search for the beyond of things and the release of spirit from matter will have to be balanced by a new concentration upon the building of cultural forms and of adequate instrumentalities for the controlled use of the immense powers modern civilization has released. And this means, first and foremost, the development of a new type of womanhood.

It is woman's function to bear these instrumentalities for control. The organism of a child is an instrumentality for the controlled release of life and spirit; and so is a real culture. Woman's productivity deals with the development and multiplication of all truly organic forms of culture. And as we are soon to enter an Age of abundance and of "pleniculture," woman must bring herself to the place where she becomes the very symbol of this culture of plenitude at all levels—not only the "good earth" in all its fertility, but, even more significantly, the vast sky filled with spatial immensities and countless universes.

This dualism of earth and sky is of profound symbolic significance, and it should be stressed today, for it brings much meaning to the woman ideal which must be proclaimed and incorporated if humanity is to reach a new evolutionary level of fulfillment and of peace. Dark earth filled with seed; vast sky filled with stars—both, real and productive, concrete and full. It is woman's privilege—indeed, it is her new function—to be both. And she can be both while being true to her essential and natural character. Ancient mythologies spoke of the "Virgins of Light," of the great energies of celestial Nature. We have today to understand the ideal of womanhood hidden under these celestial or zodiacal symbols; and there is much we could learn anew—if we give it a new perspective and a broader, more conscious interpretation—from the deep wisdom hidden under the Hindu concept of *shakti,* in its multiplicity of aspects.

Shakti is the great productive force of the universe. It operates in the soil of the earth, when this soil is impregnated by the nitrogen-releasing lightning. It operates in the immense spaces of our nebula, the Galaxy, in which the Ancients saw the "womb of souls." But at both levels it is productive. Woman is *shakti,* and woman can be productive in an earthly or a galactic sense. And the essential key to woman's productivity in the future "culture of plenitude" must be: *conscious expectancy.* Not the frightened expectancy of the adolescent in love with her own yearnings for an incomprehensible love, but the lucid and clearly formulated faith of the woman who shapes herself deliberately into a chalice in order to draw forth, by the power of conscious emptiness, the impregnation of the spirit *through* the man she loves.

Man and woman must act as productive agents, each in the fullness of personality. Their relationship must be given the meaning of productivity; and this, in the fullness of spiritual consciousness —not under the compulsion of an earthly and instinctual urge toward generic reproduction. This does not mean the denial of biological functions and sex. It means their inclusion within a life of total and bi-polar productivity, in which the psycho-mental type of production should eventually assume the main focus of significance. This total two-level productivity need not create an inner conflict in the woman, because, at both levels, she can remain true to her natural character; because there is no conflict between earth-nature and celestial-nature, *except when human beings are in the process of fighting their way up from earth to sky, from the unconscious compulsions of instinct to the conscious light of creative personality.*

Human beings on the whole have not gone very far "up"; but the "fighting" must cease, on a collective scale. The global pleni-culture of tomorrow will have to be established more or less at the level humanity will have *potentially* reached toward the end of this century—and perhaps of this decade—even though it will always be the privilege and the spiritual duty of individual persons to de-velop at ever higher and more inclusive levels of spiritual integra-tion and productivity. Humanity must have peace and plenitude, because it has gained as yet incomprehensibly vast power and privi-lege—the power and privilege to be God-like and to act *for and as* the universal spirit. A new culture of plenitude must learn to use under control what our modern civilization has wrought out of the Fire. This is woman's supreme opportunity—as it has been man's great opportunity to release, through the science and technology he has built, power from the core of the atom.

Woman can only fulfill her inherent function at this crucial hour of human destiny, as she foregoes the lure of transcendent phantasies and intellectual superiority, as she faces with courage, utter simplicity and humility the total realities of earth and sky in her own nature; and, having faced these realities, as she cultivates them in consecration and in love—in companionship with man, the releaser.

LOVE IN CONSCIOUS CO-PRODUCTIVITY

Modern science has brought to our present generations techniques of production sufficient to meet at the physical level all conceivable needs of the human race. The abundant life is before us for the taking. Yet, are men and women in the confused North America, the starving and spiritually numb Europe, the crowded lands of inchoate modern Asia, willing or ready to do the taking? Immense powers are within the grasp of men—not only of a few outstanding men belonging to an especially trained aristocracy, but of the average educated man. Yet the hands which might grasp these powers can hardly un-bend; the minds, which could adjust to the obvious requirements of a world-situation overflowing with promises of total abundance and happiness, are rigid with fears and conflicts. Men are blinded by ghostly images and obsolete goals. They have the tools for production. They "wish" they might produce. But no man can bring forth a harvest out of the substance of his inner or outer universe unless he has had the vision—however dim—of what could be produced, and the faith—however unsteady —that it can be produced. Most men and women today have neither such a vision nor such a faith—*because they do not see themselves essentially as productive personalities.*

For over a century, and even since the Renaissance, men and women have sought with compulsive and mostly blind determination to become "individuals." They have sought freedom from the soil; they have flocked to big cities. They have deserted the fields, where seeds are grown through the wholesome cooperation of men and universal life, for huge factories and assembly lines. There they repeat endlessly and automatically set operations with no sense of vital participation in the total rhythm of industry. Men and women have become smooth little cogs and bolts, pieces of

97

wires and hollow tubes in the, to them, incomprehensibly complex and vast Machine of national production. The Machine as a whole produces — enormously, wantonly, meaninglessly. The men and women whirling, pounding, chemistry-making within this Machine, in spite of all their motions, do not "produce." The gestures they make are aimless; in the sense that cashing a weekly check is no real or significant human *aim,* but only an automatic social necessity, like feeding or cleaning oneself.

Men and women have become, or try hard to become, "individuals"; each an indivisible unit. But indivisible units, *as such,* do not produce. They only act out their supposed (and constantly challenged) indivisibleness in order to perpetuate it jealously against anything that would encroach upon its abstract character and abstract rights. Men and women move together in crowded cities; they room together, they eat together, they do not "combine"—even in love. They are not "more" by being together; in most cases, they are "less" than by being alone. They take from each other; some may give to others—but they do not consciously and creatively bring forth *value* out of their togetherness. They are always afraid to find their individualness, their rights, their sovereignty diminished! Because they have no common foundation, no root together, they can produce no seed, save on the strictly biological level. Yet even though they beget children, with them too they have no basic, impersonal common roots—only sentimental, clinging or demanding, pseudo-personal attachments. Children also have to be "individuals!"

Personality is no root. Personality can only mature and flower out of the impersonal common humanity one has shared with other human beings and under the impact of a universal spiritual Power (the inner Sun). Personality is a slowly growing product of human living and human experience consistently referred to a particular frame of reference, or ego-structure. It is product, and producer in turn. Because it has grown out of roots, it can be flower and give birth to a seed. Personality cannot be separated from productivity—from that kind of productivity which is a bringing forth, a seed-manifestation of the fullness of life that is within the living person. And—this is the essential point—fullness of life can never exist without complete relatedness with other human personalities; nay more, *without a relatedness geared to productivity*. All true relationships in which fulfilled personalities combine, and are not merely in juxtaposition, are productive. They are productive through the magic power of love; for love is that power which induces in human beings a creative state of productivity.

As productivity may operate, either in a condition of unconsciousness and of bio-psychic compulsion, or in terms of consciously determined purpose, so love may operate as an unconscious biological, social and psychological compulsion, or else as a consciously acknowledged, polarized and transfigured power, used by mature personalities in the service of a freely accepted super-personal purpose. As man and woman come to see and to evaluate one another in the light of new ideals of manhood and womanhood, as their sense of purposeful and productive participation in the social and universal Whole increases in intensity and inclusiveness, the love which gives substance and fire to their togetherness must necessarily assume a new character, a new quality. This quality should be understood and defined today as clearly and vitally, as inclusively and convincingly, as possible; for upon its cultivation and generalized expression in the new Age of plenitude will depend the fundamental quality of all basic human relationships, of marriages and social interchanges, of culture and manners. *The essential quality of any human society is derived from the quality of the love which unites its men and women.*

Love in seed-productivity, and love as consuming fire

When the tribal law operates with unchallenged instinctual compulsion—because there is no individuality as yet developed in the tribesman to challenge it—the union of man and woman is completely conditioned by bio-cultural purposes. The man tills the soil, and is happy in the feeling of muscular release of energy and of fruitful work. The man likewise "husbands" the woman's earth-nature, and is happy in sexual release and in his progeny. He is deeply attached to the productive substance he fecundates with seed—be it the dark soil or the vibrant body. This attachment is functional and instinctual; it has deep roots in the collective unconscious of all human beings. It is a compulsive force operating at a level where there is no freedom of decision or choice, no personality. It is, nevertheless, a productive force. Its one goal is the fullest possible increase of seed and substance; and, at a later stage of social evolution, of usable wares and cultured products.

When transcendent ideals begin to superimpose themselves upon the goals of biological and cultural productivity, and eventually seek to reduce the latter to a low valuation; when the devotional intensity of the mystic or the saint feeds on asceticism and subliminal ecstacies or martyrdom, then, a new type of love emerges to which is given a "spiritual" valuation. Yet such a love remains essentially a compulsive type of emotion—even though it be the love of God, or of some deified person or image. The passion for the beyond can be as tyrannical a force as the hunger for sex; its roots, as deeply submerged in unconsciousness and fate. The green leaves of a plant are drawn irresistibly to the light of the sun ("heliotropism"—from *helios*, sun, and *trope*, turning) in order that they may perform their vital function of photosynthesis (the conversion under the impact of light-rays of the carbon dioxide of the air and water into sugars and starches). In a similar manner, the devotee turns his emotional nature toward a transcendent Image in the "theotropism" of a love which aspires to capture the effulgence of divinity and to fix it in the "leaf"-substance of a humanity still far away, collectively, from the condition of mature "seed"-personality.

When, in a later period, the trend toward individualism asserts itself; when the rational intellect and its analytical outlook atomicizes society and isolates every ego from every other ego; when, as a result, personal complexes, fears and passionate yearnings toward some experience of union with, and self-loss in, others harrow the distracted soul, a new type of compulsive love develops. It is love based on psychological emptiness and need. It is the love of the Romanticist; the love of adolescent egos frightened with the responsibility of conscious and productive selfhood. It is the "erotropism" of insecure personalities seeking to warm themselves at, or be consumed by, the fire of universalized and un-personalized Eros. The initial purpose of this type of love is to stir the soul-substance into activity, to release emotional fire, to transpierce—as with lightning—the inertia of the flesh and of the unconscious earth-bound psyche. To vibrate, to feel alive and in a state of inner motion, in a flaming state: these are the needs of the adolescent type of personality—just as it is the need of the virginal soul of the devotee and mystic to experience the ecstacy of "divine love," the glowing state of self-surrender to the inrush of universal light-substance.

In both cases, the purpose of the love is lost in the thrill or rapture of the experience of love. The participants are inwardly forced into the tormenting fire, or the blinding light, of such a love. Of conscious choice, there is practically none. The individual is *in* love with love. He does not consciously perform acts of love for, and together with, another being—be the being human or divine. He does not *share,* deliberately and purposefully, his fullness with another—simply because he is not yet a mature personality, because his love is conditioned by scarcity and bondage. It is a passionate and irrational attempt to compensate for a youthful, or later crystallized, egocentricity—to burn the binding structures of the individual ego, to become free from self and one with all life; and first of all, with the beloved. And in some cases, it is a vehement re-

bellion of human beings seeking to assert their individual ego against
the tabus of tribal life or the traditions, allegiances and shams of society.

In any case, this love, which is of the nature of fire, seeks liberation and emergence into a wider realm of power and activity. It
consumes limits and boundaries; it is a revolutionary force, an emotional fervor which yearns for transcendent beyonds. It stands thus
in sharp contrast against the tribal love of men and women which
is the glow surrounding work well done in common, the natural
perfume of common accomplishment in an instinctual-cultural sense,
the happy feeling of joint participation in a collective organism,
whose structural law is unquestioned and never felt as bondage.
This biological-social love is an expression of the will to increased
productivity. It serves and glorifies the seed. The love of the Christian mystic, or of Tristan and Isolde, or of Dante for Beatrice, is
a "consuming fire" which stirs, uproots, liberates and transfigures—
or maddens—men and women craving for freedom from ego and
from social rules, yearning for the infinite sea of "cosmic consciousness."

The fire of this love surges, in most cases, from sex; but sex,
here, must be understood not in terms of seed-producing functions
as much as in terms of the release of a basic power, electro-magnetic in essence and with very strong psychic overtones. It is not
sex for the purpose of producing a progeny (procreative sex), but
sexual union as a means to overcome differentiation and the polarized state, to stir in the soul the will to merge with another in a
conquest of individual separativeness, personal isolation and loneliness. Under the burning psychic "heat" produced by this sexual,
but non-procreative, love the molecular and atomic patterns of individual selfhood become deeply altered. The personality can become "ionized," stripped of un-essentials, free to unite in ecstasy
with other individuals under the compulsive power of the energies

which surge from the common root in which all men are one in un-conscious unity.

This ego-transcending and differences-obliterating love, when finally disassociated with the last thought of sex, can be interpreted and experienced as the urge for union with the One, or, through a one, with the Whole. The transcendent lover may seek inward union with God, or an outwardly expressed communion with human-ity. But whenever the former quest reaches its goal, it always must lead to the type of life exemplified by a Buddha or Christ. He who has become one with God must assume the spiritual burdens of a distracted and earth-bound humanity. He must forever strive to transform unconsciousness and the dark compulsions of instinct into conscious illumination. He must demonstrate the radiant charity which transfigures the service of the poor or the wounded into an act of love for all mankind.

Such a compassionate love is not productive of seed; but it grad-ually releases humanity as a whole from bondage to the thought of separateness and to the seeming inevitability of conflict and war. It is a unifying power. *It integrates the essential realities of individ-uals, groups and nations by consuming in its fire the non-essentials which produce division and hatred.* It seeks to re-constitute at the conscious level of mature personalities the primordial unconscious unity of the tribe state; and to re-constitute it in total inclusiveness. Tribal unanimity was exclusive of all other tribes. But transcendent love is boundaries-transcending, culture-transcending, creed-tran-scending. Its goal is the "One World" of a truly organized, global humanity. And in this goal it finds itself a partner of modern science and technology, thanks to which world-unity has become an actual, concretely experienceable fact that no honest and intelligent man can ignore.

Science, in its multi-personal and cooperative attempts to es-tablish a body of truths acceptable to all men because self-evident, like transcendent love overcomes the rigid barriers with which traditional cultures, organized religions and racial pride have hemmed in the differentiated human collectivities. Science's techniques have built the means required for a mutual understanding and personal interchange. And science too is releaser of fire. It is the fire within the atom which will establish the foundation necessary for the integration of all peoples. And if atomic energy is destructive of antiquated structures and regressive nationalism, so is the love that is a consuming fire an iconoclastic force burning away personal crystallizations and goals made obsolete by the pull of creative tomorrows. Until man is established individually and collectively on the plane of conscious intelligence and mature responsiveness to universal creative Principles; until man has reached the spiritual status of truly individual personality, there must be destruction by fire, there must be transcendence and overcoming.

The day comes however, when, at long last, love once more operates as the servant of productivity: productivity no longer conditioned by instinctual and unconscious compulsion, no longer biological and tribal in character—but instead, the co-productivity of mature persons in and through whom God, as the "Universal Creative," acts. And the type of "seed" which this co-productivity seeks to increase by an earth-transcending kind of cultivation is an ideospiritual—or, symbolically speaking, "celestial"—type of seed: the seed of man's personal immortality, as well as the seed of a new culture established in the fullness of conscious human interchange.

Transpersonal Love

The co-productivity of mature personalities in and through whom God acts—God, the Universal Creative: these two phrases establish the only foundation upon which the new image of love may develop, which our modern humanity so poignantly needs to see exteriorized in the fabric of its marriages and of all the social activities bringing together men and women as co-participants and, potentially, as "companions." These phrases may have a mystical ring which makes them sound strange and elusive, or meaningless, to the modern intellectual of either sex. Yet they refer to the deepest realities of human consciousness and human love. These realities, any one can fathom their meaning who has relinquished his or her reliance upon the superficialities or the transcendent idealism of a society yearning for fullness of life while, at the same time, opposing incessant obstacles to the inrush of power and vision which alone can give man fulfillment, peace and the sense of participation in immortal values.

There is "co-productivity of mature personalities" when man and woman come together as individual persons in order deliberately to perform, in fully conscious cooperation and love, productive activities. This is production *from* personality; whereas the instinctual, unconscious production of man and woman bound to bio-psychic patterns of behavior and feeling—or helplessly driven by their yearning to transcend and deny these patterns—is production *toward* the eventual attainment of mature personality. The state of truly mature personality, however, is never realized until the individualized person is able to relax what C. G. Jung called graphically "the cramp in the conscious," and to accept the transpersonal way of life; until the individual person, whether man or woman, overcomes the tightness of an ego haunted by the preoccupation of keeping its structure so rigidly what it is, that it finds itself completely shut to any influx of power.

A truly mature personality operates within the structural framework of a relaxed ego. The center of this relaxed ego is able and eager to open to the downpour of universal energy and ideo-spiritual realizations. In another sense, it is like a crystal-clear lens through which the vast tides of the universal mind are brought to sharp focus and given *operative form* as ideas and words, as emotionally stirring Images and symbols. The first alternative—*the open centrum*—, if not taken too literally, pictures what the transpersonal way means basically for a woman who is a conscious in-

dividualized person. The second alternative—the crystal-clear lens
—gives a clue to the inner nature of the man who has reached a
similar level of development.

In both cases, the essential fact is that the universal spirit is able
to act *through* the individual ego, to permeate the total organism of
personality with the purpose and the power of God. This purpose
and power of God, in reference to human beings, constitute what
we have called "Man" and "celestial Nature" (the latter, in contrast to "earth nature").

We defined Man as the central theme of all human evolution, of
which all individual "I's" are particularized variations; as the seed-
hood of humanity manifesting through the many seed-men. And by
"earth nature" we refer to unconscious, instinctual and compulsive,
bio-psychic productivity; which we may now symbolize under the
name of Eve: earth-bound motherhood. (The haunting pull of
sexual desire, the fascination of the *femme fatale,* Lilith, who like
a whirlpool draws into an abyss of disintegration all that has form,
name and meaning, being the negative aspect of this earth-nature.)

As to celestial or divine Nature, the very concept of it has been
so clouded or sentimentalized by the idealistic transcendentalism of
Christian thought that it has acquired a dream-like character. There
can be no real understanding of the creative process at the level of
mind and ideas until this dream-like quality is superseded by a very
realistic and concrete, *yet super-physical,* characterization. To call
this divine Nature "higher Nature" is to establish a rather unfor-
tunate negative or pejorative meaning for earth-nature, which becomes then "lower nature"; yet, between the "ideo-creative" (celestial) and "body-procreative" (earthly) aspects of human energy
there is what can be adequately called a difference of level.

Procreative energy is energy operating as producer of earth-born
physical organisms. The creative energy which, on the other hand,
is the substance of celestial Nature is productive of another kind
of "organisms" functioning at the level of mind, ideas and ego-

structures. These "organisms" are transcendent, yet *when they are completely formed and integrated* they are concrete and real. But this can only occur when the mental structure, the abstract concept, the potential form of selfhood are indissolubly "mated" with a definite portion of celestial Nature. When form is integrated with energy, an organism is produced; not before.

This basic principle must never be forgotten. By forgetting it, or twisting it out of its real field of application, or misapplying it, European culture has lost her way. There can be no "culture of plenitude" (as we defined it in terms of total multi-levelled productivity) unless the meaning of the impregnation of divine energy by ideo-spiritual forms is clearly understood. And mankind will not understand it as long as it does not modify its image of God so as to make it include the two poles of *any* type of productivity, form and energy—which means, at the "higher" level of human activity, idea (or logos) and spiritual power.

The ancient religions of the vitalistic ages understood well, in their own way, this bi-polar character of the Deity. They worshipped God in two aspects; as the Father and the Mother, as *Shiva* and *Shakti* (in the Hindu *Tantras*)—which meant, when philosophically explained to Initiates, as the spiritual essence of consciousness or mental activity, and potency or power. They avoided the difficulty of an absolute kind of dualism by adding that, in a state of transcendent being, consciousness and bliss, the Father and the Mother are utterly one. However, as soon as cosmic manifestation begins and the universal Void becomes filled with substance-energy, the Father—it is said—withdraws in a state of latency, after having impregnated the Mother with the Idea and Plan (logos) of the new universe. From then on the Mother constitutes the divine substratum of all that is and will be. The divine Potency—once impregnated with the divine Logos-Idea—differentiates into all the many powers on which the universe operates as a vast cosmic organism. Each of these powers fits into the universal Plan, and provides the foundation for one of the multitude of types of consciousness, of biological species, and of human beings.

In man, the latent Father—asleep, as it were—can be reawakened and made to reunite with the Mother; that is with the *unified* energies of the total bio-psychic organism. This means "liberation," utter bliss, universal consciousness—the reconstitution, in and through man, of the transcendent state of divine unity: Father-Mother in indistinguishable union.

Christian theology differs far less from the above, in its cosmogony and its concept of the Creation, than it might seem from the popular way in which it is expressed. One of the main differences is that—long before the time of Christ—the divine Mother-principle had become transformed by the religious seers of Israel into the "Spirit of God" that moves over the waters of Chaos (Genesis I). Woman had lost the stature which she once had, at a time when all human productivity centered around biological activities. She had become the Eve, mated to an earthly Adam; both being bound to the earth and the cultivation of seeds. In the meantime the "creative God" (Elohim) of the first chapter of Genesis had become the "Lord God" of the *second* chapter of Genesis, the divine power of organic formation and psychic personalization, Ieve or Jehovah.

The *first* Biblical Creation is a spiritual one, operating in the world of ideas and souls, of archetypes. The secondary Creation of Adam and Eve in the garden of Eden refers to the birth of our present humanity involved in the toil of the Age of scarcity, in the particularisms, the fears, the lacks, the jealousies, the ill-will born of bondage to a particular geographical environment and climate. It is to "redeem" humanity from the curse of this Age of scarcity that Christ comes (symbolically or literally) to give to all men "life more abundant"—to give the "living waters" which never dry out, the "living bread" from Heaven, eating which the individual knows death no longer; while the men who feed on the "manna" (intellectual mind limited by the ego) in the desert (general scarcity) are forever in bondage to death.

All that Christ brought to the new humanity is epitomized and synthesized in the Holy Spirit, the Spirit of truth and understanding, the Comforter that comes down "from the Father" (divine consciousness) to sustain the disciples of the Logos. These are the Companions "all of one mind," who, united in "the upper chamber" of man's conscious being, receive the knowledge of the universal Plan destined to unify all men through the magic of the one Purpose—and the power to serve effectively the realization of that Plan.

The Holy Spirit which descends upon the Apostles as "tongues of fire"—the power of the Word—is the counterpart of the "spirit of God" that creates the world according to the first chapter of Genesis. In both cases what is meant is divine Nature, or divine Potency—the feminine pole of the Creator. *It is this divine Nature to which the new woman who lives according to the transpersonal way can open herself. By so doing she becomes a fit companion for the seed-man in the creative ritual of total conscious productivity.*

Through the "open centrum" at the core of the woman's conscious and individualized personality the potent tide of the Holy Spirit flows. Through the "crystal-clear lens" at the core of the man's ego the creative Logos — God's Purpose, i.e. Man — is focused as a formulated idea, an operative structure (blue-prints and schedule of work). As the man and woman unite their being in the ritual of a consciously all-inclusive, transpersonal love, the creative union of the two poles of Deity is accomplished in act. It is accomplished *through* the love of man and woman.

This love is consciously co-productive—not compulsive and unconscious. It is not rooted in bio-psychic instinct. It is instead a deliberate answer to the need of humanity, *whatever this need might be.* That which answers through the united man-woman is the spirit, the creative "emanation" of God; and this spirit-emanation is bipolar. It is logos and potency, idea and force, vision and the energy to stamp that vision upon society which has called for it in its need.

At the bio-psychic level male and female are brought together, under the compulsive thrust of instinct, to provide a bi-polar agency through which Life can operate. Man and woman, in such a type of union, act as *carriers of ovum and sperm*—not as individual persons. Even when the purely instinctual act develops potent overtones of feelings, of personalized emotions and ideals; even when passionate love surges as an all-consuming flame from the furnace of aroused sex and seeks to deny its biological source; even then, unless artificially blocked, the meeting of sperm and ovum occurs under the control of the impersonal generic Life that animates the human species and assures its perpetuation in spite of personal human wishes or superficial plans. Life is the Actor through men and women unaware of its plans.

At the ideo-spiritual level, Life is superseded by the divine Creative Spirit. In and through the consecrated man and woman who consciously and purposefully unite their beings, in order that the need of humanity might be answered and their voluntarily assumed shares in the great purpose that is Man might be completely fulfilled, this divine Spirit acts. In that creative act of the Spirit, through the man and the woman, love reaches its most perfect expression. It is, then, divinity in act. God, the Eternal Productive, *is* love—love, not as a vaguely idealistic sentiment or feeling of unity, or a poignant burning passion that yearns for unattainable ecstasy of self-forgetfulness and transcendent bliss, but love as a clear creative answer to the need of the world.

Spirit, indeed, is always a creative answer to the need of the world. Creation is not a "play"—as Hindu philosophers who sought to react against the functionalism and totalitarianism of the Brahminical society would have us believe. Creation is God's answer to a world in chaos, to the need of that which has come to experience only disintegration and the atomicism of matter utterly un-illumined by spirit. Creation is a perpetual re-establishment of universal Harmony. It is an act of integrative Ideation by the divine Intelligence that is absolute Harmony.

Man and woman can partake in this ever renewed act of divine Creation, consciously and in the full productiveness of their total humanity. They can do so, in an incomplete manner, as single personalities, because in every individual person the whole of the universe and the full essence of divinity is latent. Yet, in order to bring that which is latent and only potential to a condition of total actuality and complete efficiency, the individual person must reach, beyond the boundaries of his ego, to those with whom, in interdependence and joint consecration, he can perform the ritual of the Spirit. Man reaches toward woman; woman reaches toward man. And both man and woman can know themselves as participants in a vast Company of consecrated persons who, together, are building out of the root of man's common humanity the ultimate and global Seed, Man. In that Man, God's creative purpose is fulfilled, in so far as humanity on this earth is concerned. In that Man, the divine Logos is made fully concrete, and the power of divine Nature is condensed—as in the seed, archetypal structure and potency of life are combined . . . the two polarities of the Eternal Productive.

The Love of the Open Eyes and the Light-between

If such be the ultimate goal for the love of man and woman, how can the present-day men and women of our confused and materialistic civilization work toward the realization of such an ideal? It must seem indeed a far distant ideal to anyone well acquainted with the character and inner quality of modern loves and modern marriages! And yet contemporary psychology and psychotherapy, in their most significant attempts, are clearing a path toward its realization; clearing it through the jungle of human selfishness and pride, of woman's excitement with newly-won social freedom and education, of man's concentration upon social and material success in a purely individualistic sense.

It is an often terrifying or bitterly disappointing task. The psychologists who are seeking to perform it, the new philosophers or "spiritual leaders" attempting to provide for it a foundation of universal principles, even the artists who, in usually unconscious and semi-mediumistic ways, formulate symbols of human integration or hope to arouse men and women from their taken-for-granted ruts of feeling by projecting ghastly images of social and personal decay—all these men are reaching or groping toward a solution of the problems of human relationship at the historically new level of conscious and individual personality. The aggressive feminism of many disappointed or frustrated modern women, the exaggerated and out-of-focus sensibility of men emasculated by matriarchal and possessive love or frightened by the cold materialism of their fathers and the world of business, the juvenile delinquency and criminality of youths who fit nowhere and thus act everywhere as disintegrative anarchists: all these primarily psychological phenomena of our incoherent society are founded upon the failure of individualistic men and women to live lives of harmonious and creative relationship.

The ancient foundations of strictly bio-psychic and instinctual man-woman productivity have been nearly shattered or twisted beyond all inspiring meaning. The new goal of conscious co-productivity and clear self-dedication to the fulfillment of the need of humanity is not even dimly envisioned, except in the rarest of cases. Unconscious tribal fertility is demonstrated mostly in the slums, where nothing makes sense—and least of all the perpetuation, through uncontrolled propagation, of such human conditions! Elsewhere, as aimless youngsters meet in abortive or peripherical contacts, as bourgeois men and women indulge in automatic gestures without radiance, beauty or vital meaning, love is overshadowed by the "war of sexes" and the conflict of personal complexes born of fear and inner scarcity.

Transpersonal love, love in clarity of human understanding and in the light of spiritual vision, love utterly consecrated to a super-personal purpose—such a love demands of its men and women much that neither, as a rule, is willing to give. Above all, it requires an unceasing state of watchfulness and objectivity. And it is such a state which we seek to symbolize here when we write the phrase: the love of the open eyes.

God, in ancient symbolism, is often represented by the never-closed and lidless All-Seeing Eye, for the essence of divinity resides in the absolute continuity of a consciousness that not only sees everything but never indulges in the unconscious state of sleep. The new love, likewise, should not only be aware of all that, within the lovers, strives for expression and fulfillment, or hinders these, but should seek never to lapse in unconsciousness and automatism, to slide into the shadow-state of inattention and of meaningless habit.

In the "love of the open eyes", the man's yearning to lose himself in the warm unconsciousness of woman's psychic motherhood should find no place. Gone also should be woman's tendency to day-dreaming, to the vague idealism in which love appears as a fairy tale and the kiss of the Prince Charming is the only cause for awakening from the long unconsciousness of the biological state—an awakening which actually means, ordinarily, but the projection of a dream-image upon the actual man. But the man is a very concrete fact, and the realities of love—psychological even more than biological or practical—only too often tear to shreds the beautiful image of the dream-lover. Or should the woman hold in her unconscious a father-complex which forces upon her husband or lover the image of all the remarkable virtues with which she endowed her father—or which, for lack of a father, she associated with her future beloved—then again the concrete husband with whom she is now sharing actual problems, privations and struggles for growth cannot, as a rule, fit the dream-picture.

All such psychological attitudes bring to love, and especially to the daily performance of all that is required of married life, a sense of confusion, of hesitancy, of fear and discouragement or boredom. These can be dissipated only through an extreme of inner wakefulness, through a complete willingness to face everything that in oneself hinders or deviates the flow of love, the stream of spiritual purpose and significance; a complete willingness to face the beloved and his or her problems, to see him or her in reality, in truth and in understanding, without the compulsion of superior attitudes or the subtler pull of motherly compassion.

Total wakefulness, constant watchfulness, clarity of vision and charity in understanding; and always burning between the two companions, as they face each other, the light of super-personal purpose. In and through an all-human purpose, we have seen that individual freedom of personality and total productivity for all and by all can be reconciled, in actuality, within the social life of humanity. It is the fire of an intimately experienced purpose, as it burns steady and lights the individual personalities of united men and women, which gives strength and vital effectiveness to that social reconciliation. Society begins in the love of its men and women. It is illumined by the warm and clear loves of those who consecrate their togetherness to the creative fulfillment of its ultimate purpose, Man.

In this seed-consummation of human evolution every component factor must not only be fully alive, awakened and significant, it must be *pure*. And by "purity" we mean the quality of being fully and solely what one is according to one's individual identity. Purity, thus understood, is almost synonymous with inherent necessity— not the false "necessity" of the opportunist who forever compromises with circumstances and justifies himself by claiming "It was necessary to do this or that . . "; but the true necessity which is an expression of spiritual purpose and of the transpersonal state in which the personality is a mouthpiece or a lens for the spirit to project itself through.

Purity is also to be understood in terms of the intrinsic nature of whatever power an individual is using. The intrinsic nature of the power used must always determine the character of the act of release, and of the "engine" through which the release occurs. This we saw, when discussing the problem of full productivity in an adequately built culture. We pointed out that as man and woman use two distinctive and indeed complementary types of creative energies, their personalities need be different and polarized to each other.

This is obvious in terms of biological procreation; but it is just as true in terms of conscious creative action at the ideo-spiritual level. This level is that of the *creative mind*—which must not be confused with the *associative intellect* which only synthesizes sense impressions into generalizations and concepts. Creative mental activity implies dynamic polarization; and this means that on that level also man must be masculine and woman feminine. In transpersonal love and transpersonal living *polarity runs clear through the whole personality,* whether of woman or man. In this consists the state of true inner purity. Each lover is "purely" what he or she is. In their bi-polar integration at all levels spirit finds a focal field for its activity.

Here however, we are once more confronted, within a somewhat different frame of reference, with the characteristic dualism or dilemma already discussed: on one hand, the ideal of a complete self-sufficient personaltiy (a "microcosm") in which all energies and functions are activated; and on the other hand, the ideal of effective productivity, whether at the biological or the mental-spiritual level.

As the emphasis is placed by a society or culture upon the "individual", as this individual is considered as an absolute and an end in himself, able to develop in at least relative isolation and with no real necessity for human interchange (except as a matter of convenience and perhaps self-indulgence), then, the logical consequence is for every person, male or female, to seek fulfillment, either in an ideal bi-sexual (hermaphrodite) state of self-containment and self-sufficiency, or else in a transcendent condition of overcoming of sex and polarity.

If, on the contrary, a society stresses the goal of full productivity, primary attention is logically placed upon the power (and the instrumentalities for the release of this power) which production requires. Every producing person must use that type of power which the person is best fitted by nature to handle with full efficiency. As production in anything like a large and effective scale obviously requires the cooperation of various types of productive mechanisms and of energies, this means that producers with various types of congenital or specialized abilities must work in close correlation; indeed, in a state of functional interdependence. And this is true, whether the emphasis upon productivity is placed at the instinctual level of biological procreation (when a tribe or a nation seeks to increase its population for one reason or another), or at the social level of agricultural and industrial production, or at the ideo-spiritual level of mental creativeness. In every case the instrumentalities used for production must be efficient and clean; the character of the power they use must be clearly defined, well directed. unadulterated and concentrated for greatest effectiveness.

In the first above stated instance (where individual fulfillment is a dominant goal) the ideal of the masculine-feminine Hermaphrodite is likely to prevail wherever men and women seek to reach beyond the state of instinctual bio-psychic unconsciousness and into that of individualized consciousness and independence. In the second instance, the ideal of fullness of productivity for all and by all conditions the growth of a sense of human interdependence—which is, at the level of man-woman intimate relationships, love. But this productive mature love can only be reached step after step, in most cases.

The Hermaphrodite ideal is energized by self-love, or in psychological terminology, narcissism. As narcissism breaks down under the pressure of psychic and glandular urges, the next step is homosexuality—love without what seems then the "taint" of productivity, love without responsibility or without objectivized activity through organs used according to their natural power-releasing characteristics. A stage further is the self-indulgent love of adolescents (whatever their actual age); of men and women who, while more or less normally active at the physiological-sexual level, become related to each other *at the psychological level* in a non-objective, non-productive and confused manner. They still love themselves narcistically each in the other; they project upon each other that part of their nature which they cannot, or shrink from, consciously acknowledging. This irrational, unconscious, and usually anti-social or a-social, part of the nature of the lovers is the contrasexual part: the feminity of the man (or, as Jung calls it, the "anima") and the masculinity of the woman ("animus"). It is energy not differentiated for consciously productive use either in the body or in the psyche, but instead repressed and purposeless—energy which keeps the consciousness enthralled and blind.

When an individual person speaks of being both masculine and feminine, with the intent of glorifying himself or herself as one demonstrating "completeness of creative being", the bare fact is that such a person merely seeks to glamorize a condition which is primarily negative, emotionally unsteady and haunted by the lack or fear of productive fulfillment. This condition is the result of childhood inhibitions, adolescent frustrations or illness, and perhaps inadequate glandular functioning. It may lead, in due time, to a rich personality; but only *after* a long process of reorientation of energies climaxing with the awakening of the creative spirit within. In the meantime, the emphasis upon individualism and isolated self-containment (or even sheer selfishness and greed) results in the inability (perhaps tragically felt and desperately compensated for) really to experience love.

Relatedness, creative productivity, love are inseparable terms. But they may all operate at the level of unconscious instinct, or at that of conscious individualized intelligence in mature personalities. In the first case, they are blind—like the Greek god Eros. In the second case, they are guided and directed by "open eyes" that, lucidly and objectively, *see*. The "love of the open eyes" is love with vision, and with conscious purpose. And it is love within the field of a light that absorbs all shadows and dissipates all psychological "projections" and mirages. How does a photographer dispose of unsightly shadows on a face he is to portray? He focuses upon this face two or more beams of light. Similarly, under the lights that steadily shine from the consciousness of each lover, all shadows are absorbed; all negativeness is assimilated. In mutual trust, all fears vanish.

The "reconciliation of the opposites"—total individual fulfillment in independent self-sufficiency, and interdependence in joint productivity—is effected through the "love of the open eyes". It is effected because the contrasexual elements in the personality which, of themselves, could only operate in an unconscious and undifferentiated condition while balancing the differentiated and conscious energies of the ego, reach through this love a state of clarity and purposeful meaning. The negative undeveloped feminity of the man discovers its productive function as it blends with, strengthens, yet is illumined by, the positive and mature feminity of the beloved woman. The negative undeveloped masculinity of the woman likewise is given its true function as it blends with and is grounded in the objectively and positively active masculinity of the man.

More than this: as the man and the woman leading the transpersonal life become consciously linked with, and agents for, the universal spirit in its twofold character as creative selfhood (or logos) and infinite potency (or "celestial" Nature), the femininity of the man becomes in-spirited by this celestial Nature *through* the woman he loves, and the masculinity of the woman becomes structured and attuned to God's purpose ("Man") *through* the beloved man.

This is the one way to a complete illumination and arousal of the entire personality of either man or woman by the universal bipolar spirit. It is the way of transpersonal love that manifests in full openness of vision, in lucid consciousness of total being (self and potency, idea and energy, form and animating substance). In this way only, the goal of full productivity operating through well focused and thoroughly efficient organs of release of power, and the goal of integral personality in conscious and free individualization, can be reconciled. *This transpersonal love becomes thus the foundation and model for all social processes. It establishes an archetypal solution for all the basic dilemmas which rend today modern humanity.*

The symbol of such a love is a man and woman standing, face to face with eyes wide open into each others, and holding in their joined hands a flame. This flame, burning between them at the center of the web of bi-polar energies activated by their love and by their joint consecration to the work of the Spirit, emanates a light that not only floods their harmonized beings, but radiates through the whole world of Man. It radiates over this wide world because, in this flame, God finds a focus for spiritual action; through it, the archetypal seed of an Age of conscious plenitude and joyous productivity is given power in the realm of human lives; by its light, the society of tomorrow can distinguish its new goals and strive to pattern itself upon the divine Word that alone will fill its need and feed its hunger for reality and for bread.

Harmonizing the Opposites
in Our Global Society

A NEW TYPE OF HUMAN BEINGS
FOR A NEW SOCIETY

Why do human beings live in a state of society? Very few persons ever find it necessary to ask themselves this question. They take human society for granted, just as they take for granted the human body, its functions and the mysterious alchemy by which consciousness and intelligence emerge from the experience of living. They say: "I am tall, I am strong, I have blue eyes and a heart which beats"—just as they say: "I am a Hindu. I am a Jew. I have a King or a Constitution. My people is great. My country". The ordinary human being does not question these facts. He does not question his instincts, his life-wants. He lives in them. He has always lived in them. He has always sought their fulfillment, the way of happiness in them. Except in times of deep upheaval and collective crisis. Except when, fired by the power of stirring ideas preached by strangely compelling individuals, human beings have been urged to rebel against the taken-for-grantedness of their bodies and their societies, their instincts and their kings. They then have denied these; they have fought against them; they have gone far and away, in search of gold or God, in search of New Worlds which could not be taken for granted, because they had to be consciously met, conquered, and used.

These New Worlds could not be taken for granted *at first*. Then new generations of men and women became settled in them; again ceased questioning; again identified their consciousness with the normal average rhythm of lean and bounteous crops, of good and bad Administrations, of years called happy and years of wilted hopes. And yet, however much the lives of men in these New Worlds resemble those of their ancestors in older communities, the patterns that give form and meaning to society do gradually change.

"Tribal" types of society differ indeed basically from the "democratic" types which the peoples of our modern world seek to establish or to enjoy in peace. How do they differ? Essentially in that human beings orient themselves differently to the facts and the responsibilities of social living. As the basic attitude of human beings toward their participation in their community, tribe or nation changes, so does the character of society, and all fundamental social processes also become transformed.

Any society is defined by the patterns of behavior, of feeling-response and of thinking which the men and women follow, who find their individual activities interrelated and made interdependent by the fact of social living. The historian may trace the development of these patterns to geographical and economic factors; or, if religiously inclined, he may look for transcendent spiritual causes to explain the character of social traditions and techniques in any particular society. Both approaches are true; for spirit never operates save in answer to a vital or clearly formulated need, and the leaders who establish new social patterns under a "spiritual" inspiration do so because, in their own natures and experiences, the need for them has poignantly arisen. Human needs have an economic and geographical foundation, for man can live only by using energy, and the possibility of using energy is conditioned by man's geographical and social environment. Yet the use of energy is also determined by man's level of consciousness, by man's capacity to respond to the challenges of the spirit as well as to those of material conditions, by the quality of selfhood and meaning with which he fecundates the raw data of his personal and social experience. Human needs are psychic and mental as well as economic.

Any society is defined by the essential vital needs of its members. The patterns of society change because human needs change; they remain the same in proportion as needs which are inherent in man's common humanity retain their basic character. Yet even though social patterns may remain unchanged in some of their essential features, nevertheless man's orientation toward them and the significance with which he endows them can be profoundly altered. Man's common humanity is only the foundation from which personality grows and defines its value and purpose. The story of civilization is the story of the gradual development and clarification of the relationship between personality and society, of the meaning of man's and woman's participation in the society which both moulds them and is moulded by them.

The evolution of the relationship of personality to society

Three great phases in the development of man's participation in society can be easily detected, and we can define their sequence in terms of the dialectic series of thesis, antithesis and synthesis—provided we do not forget that these three stages are all found today in our modern societies and that they refer to levels of personality-evolution which are to a great extent cumulative. A man may indeed operate at the three levels at once, shifting his attention from one to the other according to the character of the need his activities emphasize at any one time. He may have reached the highest level, but be able to maintain his consciousness, his feeling-responses and his motives for behavior focused at this level only for brief periods and only under special stress or pressure. Yet, for the purpose of analysis we have to study the three phases separately and in sequence, relating each to the typical kind of society which exemplifies such a mode of social participation in its average member.

The first stage is that in which man and woman participate in communal activities under the unconscious compulsion of instincts. They do not even "come" together; they *are together,* as shoots of a tree united below the surface of the soil by common roots. These roots are biological and physical. There may or may not be community of blood; there is always a community of need. And this multifarious need is the need to live and to multiply. A need, not a purpose. There is no individualized consciousness in it. What is conscious in it and back of it is the life of the species. There are no individuals as yet; only shoots from a common generic root. This root has absolute compulsive power over the seemingly—but only seemingly—separate offshoots. We may call this root-power: Life. We may, as men have done for long ages, entitize it as a tribal god, a totem, a Great Ancestor—or call it God, the common Father of all human beings. Names change as the level of culture and the scope of man's understanding and experience with other human beings also change. But essentially the root-power remains what it is, compelling from within as instincts do compel—an autocratic power which induces a fanatic allegiance to its decrees, and which externalizes itself into rigid dogmas or ritualistic behavior-patterns.

We have referred already in several places to this condition of human life under the name of "tribal". Actually it begins at a historical evolutionary level at which the tribe, as we usually understand this term, does not yet exist. At this level loose aggregations of undifferentiated human beings are presumably formed around the mothers and their progeny, for the protection of this progeny and in order to cope with elementary biological needs. Life rules the human beings from within his body—his blood, his glands, his sympathetic nervous system. It operates without the man being aware of this operation, and still less able to refer it to an autonomous self. The right way to act is inherent in the act; and is determined by the structure of the bio-psychic human organism. One cannot even speak of "matriarchy", because every value is contained in the immediate act; no "principle" (*arche*) exists outside of this immediate act.

The primitive human agglomerations centered around the mother becomes tribal organisms only after magic rituals and the attribution of specific value to particular methods of communal behavior establish the tribal group as a "sacred entity" with special virtues. After the successful outcome of some particular prowess in which, under the compulsion of a vital need, all the units of the primitive group instinctively acted as a unified body, a habit of action in common is built. Some one presumably comes to sense the value of this common behavior, "sees" it as a psychic fact, proclaims it as a magical solution to a recurrent need. When the need actually recurs, the memory of the previous common success is revived, projected as a visual image by a man particularly sensitive to the need and to psychic impressions. Made confident by this evocation of past success, the men go forth and win in the contest with natural enemies.

He who summoned the image of the successful past becomes in time the "medicine man". He comes to be valued as one who focuses in actual efficacity the collective power of the new group, who channels this power (*mana*) into operation. The visual revivifying of a past success before a new similar confrontation becomes a ritual—a mimetic dance. Masks are worn to stress the visual image of the successful act. He who wears the mask is taken to be the channel for power, a symbol of collective victory. And gradually a process of differentiation develops among the men of the group. "Clans" are formed, constituted by men who excel in one type of activity or another. They are distinguished by masks, signs, symbols —later, by totems. They are originally *functional groups,* and most typical among them are those connected with the use of magical power and with leadership in combat.

From being mere "life-carriers" some tribesmen emerge from this undifferentiated state into a new condition. Through "initiation", the member of a clan becomes consecrated for a *differentiated* type of performance of work; he thereby becomes also the mouthpiece or "medium" of the god who represents the bio-psychic source of a new type of power. The initiated tribesman, as holder of an office, is a *personage*—i.e. the wearer of a mask. As human evolution proceeds he will become an individualized *personality;* no longer an integral part of the unconscious tribal whole, but one who seeks to control "magical" powers produced by collective tribal action to the end of acquiring individual prestige and power for his own use and for the perpetuation of clan, then class, privilege.

As the process of social differentiation unfolds, a new type of participation in the collective life of society becomes evident: participation for the sake of increasing distinctions between human groups, then human individuals. The phase of "antithesis" has been reached. A few men seek—first without conscious intent and as a matter of emergency-need, then deliberately—to place themselves in such a position with regard to society that the social mass and its average character become like a pedestal on which they can stand in eminence and isolation. Why should they thus become set apart? Simply in order to be able to evolve specialized traits and abilities, without the first faint traces of these being quickly absorbed back into the racial average.

This process of separation and specialization is an evolutionary process. It *must* take place, and the men who start on this dangerous but necessary road to eventual full individualization are the agents of human evolution—and of God in His aspect as "the Adversary", as the cosmic source of all antithesis, as that power which establishes the need for the concrete manifestation of the Son out of the unmanifest, utterly transcendent Father-Mother unity. Consciousness in the world of objective being resulting from differentiated activity, these men, who appear as destroyers of tribal unanimity and peace, actually initiate the process that will give, in due time, objective knowledge, mental skill and above all individual freedom of choice to all human beings. Ancient religions depict them as "rebels" as "enemies of the gods", as "Lucifers". They are strife-makers; but also "bearers of light" (*Luci-fer*)—of the light of conscious, individualized intelligence.

Privilege signifies literally the establishment of "one's own law" (from *privus,* one's own, and *lex,* law). When initiatory clans begin to appear within the tribal community in order to train groups of men especially efficient in some phases of social productivity (war-making, magic, etc.), these clans establish gradually laws of their own, distinct from the basic organic law of the tribe. The laws or rites of the clans, however, are not fundamentally in opposition to the common law that is inherent in the structure and instincts of the tribe as a whole; no more than the specialized function and rhythm of the liver or the heart develop in opposition to the law of the entire organism in which these organs participate.

Maximum productivity requires division of labor, organic differentiation and the proper spacing of the several interrelated organs or social groups. At the tribal stage this organization of productive work is simple, direct and determined by the compulsive power of a need evident to all members of the community. It involves theoretically no conflict. The special law of the functional group is felt and understood as an integral part of the organic law of the community. Privilege, in the present day characteristic sense of the term, arises however when the law of one group, class or individual acquires its significance at the expense of the welfare of the whole community; when it ceases to be the privilege to participate in the whole life of society according to one's own most developed ability and in terms of the fullest, most harmonious, productivity of the whole; when it becomes, instead, the privilege to set oneself *apart from* the whole in order to develop oneself without reference to the welfare of the whole, or at the expense of the whole.

Privilege, in this antithetical sense, means a *negative* participation in society. The absentee landlord, who extracts rent from the peasants producing foodstuffs in the fields while he spends money at some princely court for show, participates negatively in the productive life of society—and the modern wealthy capitalist, who develops complexes and a neurotic ego in New York's Park Avenue while fed by the interests of his inherited stocks and bonds, does likewise. However, these social types are not the only ones to participate negatively in society. Negative participation does not mean always the destructive or predatory use of social privilege. It can be highly constructive in an evolutionary human sense in so far as it can mean the development of individualized consciousness, of self-will, of freedom of choice, and of all the transcendent powers latent in man.

Ascetic monasticism and the social isolation of the Hindu Yogi constitutes in appearance rebellion against (or escape from) the social law of biological productivity. Man, by such ascetic un-social practices, denies his instincts, destroys the unconscious harmony and happiness of natural living in his personality. To what end? To the end that he may become free from the unconscious compulsions of society and human nature, from bondage to human needs, to social patterns of material production—and even to the rituals of organized religions—; to the end that he may become a *single* personal manifestation of divinity, complete and secure in his own identity; an "individual," indivisible and one. To ask spiritual privilege is to ask to live according to one's own individual law in the spirit; or according to the law of a spiritual elite related fundamentally to transcendent God, but not to human society in its constant interdependent productive activities. And the men who claim the right to such a life may serve humanity by developing the new powers and the new sense of self which is absolutely necessary for the *ultimate* realization of a fully individualized personality.

The "rugged individualist," the adventurer, the Romantic individual who dramatizes himself and his breaking of conventions or traditions (and perhaps laws) in the name of his "genius," are also men who (in some cases at least) contribute to humanity by refusing to participate normally and organically in society. Even a disease can contribute to the ultimate wealth of organic living; and many men have reached greatness and have brought great gifts to their people because of a strong inferiority complex, or of some injury they inflicted upon their own organism. And the adventurer revolting against the, to him, binding and stifling laws of small community living may end by bequeathing an empire to the very people against whom he rebelled and perhaps by whom he was cursed for his anarchistic ways!

In brief, during the second phase of the participation of man in society, we find man establishing his individuality against, or in denial of, the very nature of society. He gains independence by revolting against the typical instinctual organic interdependence of tribesmen within the tribal whole. He develops his ego out of frustration, pain and tragedy; by repressing or denying his natural desires and functions. He finds his self in opposition to society—or he finds "God" in opposition to human nature.

This stage of antithetical participation in society is, however, only a means to an end. Of itself, it has no meaning. Likewise the long millennia of what the Hindus call the "Age of the four castes" and Karl Marx "the Class Struggle" have in themselves no meaning, save as a means gradually to develop in human personalities differentiated characteristics, mental objectivity and a clear focus of individual selfhood, as autonomous factors independent of earth-conditions. Any antithesis links the synthesis to the thesis, and is indeed a *negative presentiment* of this synthesis, the values of which it serves to establish, at least as a negative film of the ultimate reality. Thus, in truly significant religious symbolism, the Devil serves the purpose of God. He forces God to *actualize* Himself on earth into His Son, as a model or prototype which all men eventually will emulate—thus becoming God-like, as is and always has been their inherent destiny. Yet this "service" proffered by the Devil to God is an unconscious service. Consciously, the antithetical ego denies his God. But when this individual and separative ego comes finally to realize that he served all the while that against which he bitterly rebelled and ranted, he begins to "assimilate" to his consciousness the long denied social values and natural energies *with reference to their ultimate meaning in God*—which means, with reference to what they can bring to the fulfillment of Man.

This psychological process of assimilation by the ego of unconscious social-natural elements is the "individuation process" described by C. G. Jung; and it should not be confused with the psychological process of "individualization" through which the ego emerges as a separate and differentiated structure of consciousness from the matrix of the tribe, in which it existed in latency and unconsciousness. Individuation, in the Jungian sense of the term, is the process that leads to the full integration of the personality not "apart from" society, but "as a consciously contributing part of" society. Through this process, man defines his participation in society. When a sufficient number of individuals have re-oriented themselves toward this goal of conscious, free, responsible and productive participation in society, the structures of society are changed. At first, however, the change is theoretical far more than actual. Accepted as an ideal and recorded in official documents, it is circumvented by the many men and groups who cling to the antithetical concept of privilege—even when the evolutionary justification for this separative and proud attitude, in the name of the preservation of specialized traits and cultural values, has lost its one-time validity.

It is at this point that our present-day society stands, historically speaking. The principles of "democracy" have been established at an abstract eighteenth century level. The tremendous powers released during the last hundred years by science *could* have given concrete substantiation to these principles. Society could have been utterly transfigured. But several capital factors introduced difficulties and put grinding brakes to the process of transformation.

First was the fact that the men who were in position to use and take advantage of the new powers of industry and commerce had been trained, for generations, according to patterns of separative and aristocratic privilege — patterns based on the one-time obvious physical as well as spiritual scarcity. These men refused to—and psychologically, as a rule, *could not*—readjust themselves to the new facts that: 1) there could be material advance for all, if a proper reorganization of production were effected; 2) the development of human mentality had become so rapid that it provided a *foundation* for the possibility that all human beings would act as (at least relatively) conscious and responsible personalities if given the proper education and the chance to apply its results; in other words, the fact that "spiritual" scarcity could be overcome.

These two categories of facts—and all that is derived from them at the level of personality and society—condemn today the traditional concept of *strict aristocratic segregation.* Once necessary as a means to protect the growth of newly differentiated and as yet immature evolutionary traits and faculties in humanity (as young plants are protected in hot houses from late spring frosts), this setting apart of privileged classes carrying the burden of developing *through strife a new sense* of individual selfhood has become fundamentally obsolete as a generalized social procedure. Whoever is to claim for himself the state of an "aristocrat"—of one of "the best" people—must now *prove* his claim by his power to arise from the common social foundation of all that is human, after experiencing fully man's common humanity. There is no basic social validity any longer for an aristocratic headstart in life, except in so far as a particular birth-environment and a personal heredity provide to a particular child a more cultured or more harmonious foundation for his or her development in youth. And this is because, as we shall see presently, the very substance of society has become repolarized *in principle* in terms of a new type of relationship between personality and society, which makes such aristocratic birth-privileges obsolete, because unnecessary for evolutionary purposes.

The second essential factor which made very difficult the actual realization of the abstract democratic principles of the eighteenth century has been the introduction to the realm of our Christian Western civilization of hundreds of millions of peoples who, all over the globe, had stagnated, or degenerated in by-paths of human evo-lution—and also the enormous increase of the population of the world on all continents. This sudden inrush of people into the sphere of activity of the few communities in which an attempt was made to operate society in the ways of "democracy" has tended quite obviously to intensify the desire (and in a sense the temporary need) for social isolation and aristocratic privilege at the national level. American isolationism and the restrictions placed by various coun-tries of the West upon immigration are characteristic expressions of this urge to protect the "democratic experiment" from peaceful invasion and submergence by unsteady masses of human beings— whether this unreadiness manifests in terms of unassimilatable ra-cial traits, or of stubborn religious characteristics basically antagon-istic to a truly democratic society. Likewise the eagerness mani-fested by Soviet Russia to protect at all cost her social patterns and what she also calls (not without justification) her "democracy" is due to the same cause, though the pressure against the Soviet type of society is made more acute by the direct political and ideological enmity of ruling groups in capitalistic countries.

The conflict between the Anglo-American and the Soviet worlds is based on the fear in either that the other would seek to destroy its own special approach to the ideal of a new society—or to over-whelm it by attracting the support of millions of people in Asia, Europe, Africa and South America who are still without clear-cut orientation or in an undeveloped social state. Essentially, therefore, we find two vast minority-groups (each including around 200 mil-lion human beings) seeking to preserve their new social develop-ments (and their as yet unstable and not too successful traits) on an aristocratic basis of privilege against submergence under the flood of the as yet undifferentiated portions of humanity, as well as against each other.

But what do we mean by a new society, especially by a "demo-cratic" society? Unless we can meet the issue clearly and without prejudice, we will add only more confusion to a world already groping in fear and with lack of understanding of its basic problems.

The harmonic ideal of society

The difficulty faced by modern man in giving a correct evaluation to efforts in the direction of establishing a *fully* democratic and productive world-society for responsible, mature and productive personalities is that there is little understanding of the basic difference between such a type of society and the old tribal order of life. The latter still exists in an attenuated form. Nazi Germany tried to revivify it in a mechanized and intellectualized modern version. We were horrified by its most virulent features and we realize it was a regressive—thus destructive—ideal of society; but we do not sufficiently understand that the tribal ideal still animates a definite layer of our society—and of the collective unconscious. It is something we can always revert to consciously, because it lives in every man's psychic depths, and it represents as much a phase of our psychological development in childhood (a *prolonged,* or even life-long, childhood in many cases!) as the stage of fish is an inevitable phase of the prenatal embryonic development of even the greatest human genius.

We can define a tribe as an organic matrix within which human nature (generically speaking) unfolds its latent powers, blossoms out and comes to collective cultural fruitions. Within these cultural fruitions the "seed" of individual personality develops; and as it develops, this seed gradually kills or renders obsolete the "plant" (the tribal community) from which it emerged. A truly democratic society, on the other hand, should be understood as *an associative field established in (at least relative) consciousness by more or less individualized persons in order to provide the best possible conditions for the development and fulfillment of their own creative powers and of the personalities of the men of future generations.*

This means that while a tribe operates through bio-psychic structural compulsions and in unconscious instinct *toward* the ultimate emergence of individual personalities, a truly progressive society should be established *on the foundation of* individual personality for the more or less consciously formulated purpose of promoting more complete individualization and greater personal fulfillment—in happiness and creative expression—among all its associates, present and future. Actually modern society is not only far from realizing this goal, but the majority of human beings in the world, and indeed in any one nation, are still operating at a pseudo-tribal or semi-tribal level; while, in early childhood, the "primordial We" of the tribal state is experienced by all, as the very foundation from which the development of an individual ego proceeds, either under conditions of strife and frustration (which reproduce the earlier historical phases of the "Class Struggle") or in a harmonious state of family happiness and well-being. That today children are soon regarded as "equals", as individuals who must develop self-sufficiency and the ability to make conscious moral-intellectual choices, is however a proof that, even in the sphere of the family, the tribal order is becoming increasingly obsolete. What replaces it, alas, is often a very negative antithetical state of anarchy and of personal license. But this can be blamed on the generalized greed and the destructive application of the profit motive in a society which has not yet understood how to use for the complete personal welfare of *all* its members the powers technology has released.

The ideal new society toward which the progressive minds of our day are striving is thus to be considered as a grouping of conscious individuals able to act in their own right, and to determine not only the purpose and direction of their individual lives, but—through the mechanisms of a democracy—to participate freely and knowingly in the determination of the purpose and policies of the particular communities in which they live. Thus defined, the new society and democracy are completely interrelated: there can be no real democracy where this ideal of social-personal relationship is not accepted by at least a steady and dependable majority of the people; and there can be no ultimately valid future society where some type of democratic system does not actually guarantee personal freedom of decision and of choice to its member-associates as a *sine qua non* condition of the society's existence.

Yet if, having stated this, we would go no further we would have failed to take into consideration the ultimate spiritual purpose of a society of mature personalities ready to follow what we have defined as the "transpersonal way". We would have defined a type of relationship between personality and society—a type of personal participation in society—exemplifying the pluralistic conception of spirit which, in our previous chapter on "personality," we have shown to be inadequate as an ultimate of spiritual value. There can be, beside a pluralistic type of democracy based on strict individualism, a "harmonic" kind of democracy in which individual personalities seek to fulfill the ultimate purpose of humanity as a whole by consecrating themselves as agents for the concrete realization of "Man," that is, of God's Purpose.

The ideal society, of which we now speak, has a two-fold or two-level purpose. Its immediate and operative aim is the establishment, maintenance and constant perfecting of its associative and productive techniques—i.e. of its institutions and its modes of group-operation, of the legacy of knowledge and skill which each generation is to pass on to the following generations, so that they may develop in the fullness of individual personality. But society should have also an ultimate and spiritual aim: the formation in concrete (even if transcendent) reality of the "seed of humanity", Man, in which the harvest of experience of all the persons who ever succeeded in giving their own individualized and spiritual meanings to their experiences is gathered and synthetized. This all-human "seed", Man, is a spiritual immortal reality, a *pleroma,* a creative fullness of being whence will proceed, at the beginning of some new cosmic cycle, a new spiritual Impulse productive of a new type of humanity. This all-human "seed" is constantly forming at the creative core of humanity. It is civilization and culture as one—man and woman, also, as one. It is forming from the very first time that a man having reached the fulfillment of his individual personality, in complete freedom from the tribal womb of earth-nature, refused to stop at this self-centered Nirvana and trod the "transpersonal way" as a "Son of God"—whenever, symbolically speaking, Buddha *became* Christ.

The individualistic pluralism of the eighteenth century democracy would ideally lead to a society within which individualized personalities develop in freedom and happiness, but also in intelligent and cooperative selfishness; each personality an end in itself, even while seeking to perpetuate the harmonious conditions and institutions which will make it possible for the new generations to reach likewise "individuation" and full personal fulfillment. Such a society, in contrast to our present world of tragedy, starvation and despair, will appear, it is true, as a paradise on earth. But just *because* it appears as a paradise on earth *to us now,* we should be suspicious of the ideal picture it presents. We should realize, in other words, that it is an illusory Nirvana dreamt of by desperate souls to compensate for our world-misery.

This free and happy pluralistic-democratic society should be considered as the merely "ideal" counterpart of a society based on individualistic strife and class-struggle. It is not "real", because the counterpart of an antithesis is not a real synthesis. One cannot define a synthesis merely by removing the sting and the strife from the antithesis. One cannot define an ideal democratic society by depicting a strictly individualistic society with inherent conflicts between antithetical groups, yet simply without any bitterness or violence whatsoever in these conflicts between individuals or groups. True peace is not the absence of actual war between *inherently hostile* groups. The negation of a negative makes a positive *only* in abstract mathematics. Yet because our democratic concepts are based essentially on an abstract concept of the "citizen" and of "law"—being the products originally of a typically abstract and rationalistic century—they feature this unreal mathematical operation as a human and concrete solution; and when it does not work "human nature" is blamed!

In order to bring a true synthesis, the antithesis is to be blended and reconciled with the thesis. Thus, there must be some new alchemy of the ideal of subjective tribal unanimity and of that of individualization through conflicts, objectivity and suffering, if a truly new and valid society is to be constituted. Unity is the foundation; but whereas this unity, at the tribal level, is prae-conscious and prae-individualistic, in the future society, unity must arise as the result of the fulfillment by its members of the transpersonal way of life. It is, we might say by analogy, a "transdemocratic" society. In it, unity *must be a positive factor*. Peace must be a positive factor, not only a negation of war—either through fear or through the enforcement of "law". "Law", as a rational absolute, is a typical Roman concept devised to hold in check the uncontrolled individualism of a period of social antithesis. The future society which will seek to incorporate the ideal of synthesis cannot give absolute value to "law". It will instead enthrone the concept of "harmony". The distinction between these two terms is capital. He who fails to grasp it in his own inner vital and spiritual core can never consciously become a "father" of the new society and the new humanity.

The root-meaning of the word "harmony" is: to become one, or to join in (originally, in singing together). In this "becoming one" two facts are implied: 1) there has been separation—2) the separate units have accepted a common principle of unity. In a discussion club where men agree to disagree—theoretically with the aim of becoming clearer and more objective toward the ideas they separately hold—there is no "becoming one", even when "zones of agreement" are finally defined. From these zones of agreement many other points of disagreement are merely eliminated. Unity is not attained; because nothing above, beyond, or at the center of the differences is actually recognized. To "become one" is *not* the goal, but only agreement between individuals who insist on their right to disagree, because they do not want to relinquish their sovereign right to a separate individuality. These absolute individuals may admit they are all "human beings", or "sons of the same Father"—yet, whatever unity they sense in their past *they do not project into the future as a common purpose,* as something without the attainment of which they are not completely fulfilled. They do not seek to build a society whose ultimate purpose is "harmony"; whose ultimate condition is the creative fullness of a group (or "host") of conscious intelligences that are one in creative purpose and in creative act, as all the participants in a seed-function are one in the ingathering, preserving, then releasing, of all the powers necessary to bring to birth, *through* the seed, a new plant.

In a true synthesis all conceivable antithetical factors are harmonized within the unitarian field provided by the initial thesis. In the "harmonic society" of which we speak all differentiated human traits gained through long ages of conflicts, of negation, of "sin", of self-seeking and individual acquisitiveness should become harmonized within the global field of humanity as a whole—a humanity in which individuals will (consciously and as mature, productive individual persons) acknowledge, feel and unquestionably experience the unity of Man, and in it, the active essence of the Deity. Without this vivid realization of unity, there can be no "harmonic society." But while in the tribal state men take this unity for granted as a generic, instinctual, unconscious, compulsive reality which they cannot conceivably escape or deny—because there is in them nothing to deny it with—, in the future harmonic state of society the experience of unity must, *by definition,* be a conscious, individual and freely arrived at fact of the personal life.

What place is then occupied in the scheme of human evolution by the democratic society in which there is no basic urge to reach such an experience of human unity, no social value attributed to it, no education leading to it, but instead in which the individual personality is given absolute validity, and practical agreement in the activity of these absolute individuals is reached mainly by the coercive power of laws agreed upon by the sheer weight of superior number (i.e. majority rule)? A place of transition. Individualistic democracy is a transition between the period of class and caste conflicts, and the future "harmonic society" of the Age of plenitude. It pushes the element of conflict to its extreme, by making it a competitive strife between theoretically single individuals who are ends-in-themselves and ultimate arbiters of value. By so doing the atomistic society compels, out of sheer necessity, a reaction in the direction of mutual agreement and cooperation. Thus "rugged individualism" has to turn into the Rooseveltian "New Deal". Men are forced to seek to establish "zones of agreement", by the use of social-political techniques featuring compromise, arbitration and the respect of laws passed under the principle of majority-rule. They are forced to do so within cities which are no longer "communities" but instead competitive fields; within nations still rent by class-greed and jealousy; and within a world devastated by total wars.

In polar opposition to this individualistic democracy which stresses the "divine right of the individual", it was inevitable that a social-type of approach should be sought and demonstrated in which the "divine right of the community" is emphasized and unity-at-all-cost is the keynote. The cost is usually individual freedom. And we may call this social philosophy "totalitarianism". But, if so, we must at once differentiate sharply between various kinds of totalitarianism, according to the type of unity which is being sought. It may be the *retrogressive* unconscious unity of the tribal order, *with either a biological-political or a psychic-religious emphasis;*

or it may be unity based on the only public kind of knowledge which so far has produced a type of evidence acceptable to men of various temperaments, races and cultures, viz. modern science.

This kind of unity through the common recognition of scientifically evident truths leads to a process of unification which is characteristic of our modern times; a rational unification. Modern science is undoubtedly not the last word in human knowledge, and the materialism of the average scientist or college-graduate may be a fallacious or at best a temporary and transitory phase in human development; nevertheless this does not alter the fact that the unity emphasized is a *progressive* unity, ahead of man, and for man to realize in clear, objective consciousness of purpose. On the other hand, the yearning to "return to the Mother" which many intellectuals experience after wars and defeat, and which gives new vitality and power to antiquated social and religious institutions, is a psychological compulsion implying personal and social regression—whatever it be that symbolizes "the Mother" for the frightened and psychically insecure individual. Following this compulsion, the individual *abdicates* spiritually. By seeking re-absorption into a "mystical community" and denial of individual selfhood he re-enters the womb, in a psychic sense. He gives up the evolutionary struggle toward the future society.

Anyone who fails or refuses to distinguish between the various kinds of totalitarianism *merely* because they all deny rights to the individual proves that he considers the individual as an ultimate. He who, with St. Exupery, considers that ". . . the individual is only a path. Man only matters, who takes that path" will, on the other hand, realize that the attitude toward this "Man" determines the character of the ultimate goal which the totalitarian approach seeks to reach. If a materialistic totalitarianism (such as the typical Marxian communism), by denying the basic value of the true means or "path" (the individual) for the actual manifestation of Man, fails to produce the "harmonic society" which alone enthrones Man in concrete, productive, all-human reality and truth—so also, atomistic "democratic" society, by *worshipping* this individual *and going no further,* fails.

Both fail, because both stress one pole only of the total, productive, creative substance of human society. The democracy born from Western Europe and reared in North America emphasizes the rights and the dignity of the individual personality. Soviet communism, on the other hand, emphasizes communal productivity and unity at all cost, even at the cost of individual freedom of opinion and of movement. And here again we meet our basic contemporary dilemma already discussed! In the U.S.S.R. the community-whole has nearly complete domination over the individuals-parts who are enkindled with a collective fervor, but are not "free." In the U.S.A. there is no vital sense of the community-whole, no collectively creative fervor—because the individual is considered an end-in-himself, and is free to believe, think and act as he pleases; free *for* nothing in particular, except the abstraction and the "feeling" of freedom.

On the surface the American stress upon individual freedom, unregulated initiative and unrestricted competition appears to have resulted in marvelous productivity; so that one might say that in the United States both the factors of individual personality and rich productivity have reached an optimum development. But this argument, which is heard at all times, forgets many things worth considering. It forgets the difference between the American pioneers who had centuries of European culture and mental spiritual stimulation behind them, and the Russian peasants inertially bound to their land for 2000 years of nearly Asiatic tyranny and ignorance. It forgets that the U.S.A. grew to its present size and productivity through the steady extermination and double-crossing of relatively as many Indians as there were victims in the Russian revolution, and through the "forced labor" of as many Negroes as there have been men in Siberian labor camps. It forgets that the U.S.A. got a headstart a century before the U.S.S.R. did; that the latter began with the moral and spiritual remains of centuries of feudalism and superstitions to clear away and the opposition of most of the world to overcome.

Indeed historical comparison, here, would be quite meaningless, were it not for the fact that it is being made constantly, in one way or another, and that it tends to confuse the data of the problem which the whole world is facing now. Marxian communism is a value of protest, and as such is essentially dis-harmonic. Its philosophy has been derived from the materialistic and political doctrines of German philosophers (Feuerbach, Hegel and others), from the emphasis upon the will, and upon the violent transformations this will can produce; and as well from the Messianic drive of its Jewish founder and adherents. But the "rugged individualism" of the early Spanish *conquistadores* and the North American pioneers of the frontier-days was also a value of protest, and it also stressed will, conquest, ruthlessness and the wiping out of all cultural patterns that menaced the conquerors—in this case, the Indian cultures, some of which were very advanced (in Central and South America), others which were fine models of *harmonious tribal society.*

Conscious harmony must always be born of discord; synthesis, of antithesis and differentiating strife. The essential point is that the glorification of *neither* the older atomistic and individualistic French-American democracy, nor the younger totalitarianism of the Soviets compelling the people to form a unified community "or else", can be considered as anything but a preparation for, or a transition toward, a "harmonic society". In such a society the principles of individuality and of community must become integrated. And it should be clear that the U.S.A. and the U.S.S.R. present two different, and in a sense complementary, approaches to such an integration, by stressing respectively one of the two factors to be integrated.

And yet, while this is no doubt true from an objective and dispassionate standpoint, the fact remains that the individualistic methods and institutions of Western democracy constitute—wherever they can be worked out with at least relative effectiveness and *honesty*—a more fundamental and safer approach to the realization of the harmonic society which we envision. They do so because such a society must be founded upon full consciousness and clear foci of differentiated activity, and these factors belong essentially to the individual. The individual is the "path" to tomorrow; and Western democracy serves best the needs of the individual. They outline this "path," while Russian ideology points to a social goal, which however is negated or thrown out of focus by the means used to reach it. But of what good is it to trace and embellish a path if one has no idea of the goal to which it should lead? Of what good is a new technique without a new philosophy to give it direction and purpose? If the only purpose of our Western world individuals is to be bigger and more power-full individuals, then our democracy makes no more sense than the production of bigger and speedier automobiles make sense when they are used to reach no significant place and merely to show off the skill and wealth of their makers and owners.

An individualistic democracy unable to condition its individuals so that they may live significant lives and become conscious of a super-personal purpose, whether it be called Man or God, is very close to spiritual bankruptcy. *Have we, indeed, to choose between individual freedom without significant social purpose, and significant social purpose without individual freedom?* If so, we are indeed living in an utterly tragic period.

What then is the solution? There can only be one: the birth of a new type of human being. The modern world needs desperately men and women, who, though free individuals, are utterly dedicated to the fulfillment of a significant social and all-human purpose. It needs as well men who, though comrades spiritually bound to the task of building a purposeful society, find in themselves the strength to think and to live as individuals because they have consciously identified social necessity and inner freedom. The two needs are one need, seen from Western and Eastern eyes. And that one need spells: *Service*.

The Server Type
and the management of social power

Just as one must distinguish between several basic forms of participation in society, so it is essential to differentiate between several corresponding types of service. At the level of the tribal life service is defined by the needs of the community as a whole; it is merely communal work performed under the compulsion of a vital need, unquestioned because evident to all concerned. As clans are constituted, originally connected with the performance of a certain kind of activity, as therefore the principle of differentiation of work begins to operate in society, the concept of "service" emerges in its characteristic form, as it has been known ever since. Service is being exchanged; that is, one person trained in the performance of a special kind of work exchanges the results of his acquired or congenital ability for some other social value—some other service, money or goods. And as society becomes divided into set castes or classes perpetuated and made increasingly rigid by inheritance and the principle of primogeniture, large groups of human beings see themselves compelled by birth to exchange the service they can render by reason of normal muscular strength and instinctual ability to cope with the everyday demands of agricultural production or social comfort for the mere right to exist and to multiply under some sort of protection. This protection may be assured to them by military men, or—at the psychic level—by priests supposedly able to protect from evil and disease, or from "hell fires". In either case service takes on, for long historical periods, the character of servitude or serfdom. It becomes physical slavery when victorious warriors compel the defeated to serve them as domesticated animals. It becomes psychic slavery, when a priesthood completely dominates the feelings and souls of its victims through fear and "black magic".

As the concept of the "dignity and sacredness of the individual" spreads, slave and serf disappear as official features of a class-ruled society. The slave becomes the household servant; the agricultural serf becomes the industrial proletariat. Both are theoretically free as individuals to choose their employers and their fields of service, but, in many cases indeed, this choice is entirely controlled by birth-status and race or color. It is limited by the kind of education available, by family precedents, etc.

In order to make such a condition of service more acceptable religions often extol the ideal of service by referring it to God. Every man and woman is thus told to consider himself or herself as a "servant of God"; and the priest or pope proclaims himself as the "servant of the servants of God". This transcendent glorification of service is however quite inadequate—as all transcendent values must always be—in so far as the concrete realities of the society in which it is preached fail to justify it as a basic fact. The transcendent or abstract "ideal" may be a presentiment of, and a transitory step toward, a future reality; yet this ideal has to become the vital foundation upon which the whole society is built in actual fact before it acquires the character of a truly social and personally convincing goal. To say that the Christian civilization up to now has made of "service" a valid social and personal goal because it has extolled the ideal of being a "servant of God" is merely to take hypocrisy at its face value. Until that to which service is offered becomes *a personally experienced reality,* and service means actually a concrete and productive act of evident participation in that which is being served, service cannot be realized vitally as a creative purpose by conscious and mature individual persons.

Today, however, human society has reached a stage of development at which the goal of service, by the individual to the entire community in which he participates as a creative person, not only *can* be made a concrete and poignantly real reality, but *must* become the one driving motive of individual and group action if humanity is to meet successfully the challenge of the new powers it has released during the last hundred years. But the service given by mature and inherently free individual persons to a community in which they consciously and creatively participate in terms of the gradual evolutionary fulfillment of an all-human purpose—such a service is entirely different from the actual servitude imposed by a privileged few upon undeveloped social personalities, either of the servant-class, or of the proletariat, or of the religious devotee type (psychic servitude).

First of all, it is not service to a person, family or class, but instead service to the operative whole in which he who serves participates in conscious co-productivity. Then, it is service which takes the form of *the skilled management of collective social power for the purpose of total productivity for all by all.* And in order to stress the difference between this type of service and all previous historical types, we shall name the person who serves in such a manner, a "Server". Even the connotation of biological productivity attached to this term in technical cattle-breeding terminology is not altogether irrelevant here, because this kind of service is actually a fecundative act in which society is the passive or feminine polarity, and the individual person (of either sex) dedicated to the ultimate purpose of humanity is the positive or masculine agent. A fecundative act; an act performed in the productive love of a human individual for humanity, in answer to a social need and a collective purpose.

The ideal of the server is a social ideal; it refers to man as a social person consciously participating with all other persons in the vast collective performance through which the enormous powers latent in earth-nature and in human civilization are being released and put to use. But man is also a single person. He is in himself an organic whole—a complete form of life, a particular expression of the generic powers inherent in mankind. And his spiritual responsibility to the universe and to God is to *individualize* these generic powers, to make them fully operative in a conscious, significant and purposeful way. These powers are his own, as he alone can give them individual meaning. They are for him to use as an individual, on his own responsibility.

Two basic levels of functions can, thus, be distinguished in human life: first, the *generic* level which deals with bio-psychic energies and functions (breathing, blood circulation, metabolism, muscular action, etc. and their immediate psychic overtones)— then, the *social-cultural* level which refers to all activities and powers developed through the many contacts and relationships between human beings operating within some type of social organization. Partaking of the character of both levels, sexual activities should be understood as a transition between the purely generic and the strictly social-cultural realms. In sex the generic functions reach their apex —they come to seed in the act of life-reproduction. But sex, in as much as it requires the cooperation of two persons and establishes a basic relationship between them and a progeny, should also be regarded as the very foundation of all social processes—a fact which has come vividly to light in modern psychology. Sex can be called thus a "seed-function": the consummation of one realm and the foundation of the subsequent one.

The differentiation between these two levels of human functional activities is essential, at this stage of our enquiry into the basic ideals of the new society, because to each level corresponds a particular type of energy. Each type has its characteristic meaning and value, and should occupy a definite place in the fabric of a truly "harmonic" society. In such a society the usually haphazard distinction between the individual or private and the collective or public spheres of responsibility for the use of power should become clearly defined in terms of the fundamental character of the energies operating in these two spheres.

Briefly stated, any person has the right and responsibility to use the generic powers of his organism as an individual. They came from universal life, from God. They define him as a concrete human being; he must individualize them by using them consciously and purposefully. It is his responsibility—but this responsibility is not to any other man or group of men; only to the source of these generic powers, viz. life or God. Every man must "render to God what belongs to God"—his total organism as a human being. He must give account to God and the universe for the use of this bio-psychic organism which he privately owns. He can only give account for it in his own inner being, in the sacred chamber of his heart, where the individualized personality meets his spiritual source, the God-within. Such a meeting can only occur when an individual has made the fullest possible use of his *private possessions.* And, again, these include everything with which a human being is born— all that is *latent and potential* within his total organism at birth. If one believes in the cyclic re-embodiment of a spiritual monad through a series of physical organisms, this means all the powers accumulated in these "lives" and stored in latency in the spiritual "seed" forever reconstituted—if one does not, it refers to all that is accumulated in latency within the genes of the parent cells; whatever these famous genes exactly may be!

"Public possessions", on the other hand, include the complex aggregation of social-cultural powers, wealth, traditions and knowledge which a man assimilates through education and social imitation—and all of which are the collective production of numberless persons who worked (consciously or not) toward the further development of society and human civilization. These powers, wealth, traditions and knowledge being the products of social interchange are collective in nature, and should not be considered as subject to strictly defined individual ownership. No individual has the right

of absolute ownership over them; they instead constitute *delegated social power* which he can manage, but for the management of which he is responsible to society.

The differentiation between the sphere of the strictly private possessions and of the private life, and the sphere of the public or social life is capital, because it establishes two basic realms of power and of the use of power. It differentiates the sphere of individual *management* in the name of the community and for an essentially social purpose, from that of individual *ownership* for an essentially spiritual purpose. We wrote, a while back, that society has a two-fold purpose: its immediate and operative aim is the establishment, maintenance and constant perfecting of its associative and productive techniques, institutions, etc.—and its ultimate and spiritual aim is the formation in actual reality of the "seed of humanity", Man, in which the harvest of all truly individualized experiences is synthesized and made spiritually creative. "Management" deals with the first purpose; while the use of "private possessions" (as we defined the words) refer to the second purpose.

In the tribal stage of human society, this distinction between private and public possessions does not exist, because every form of power usable by man is understood as an expression of "life"— and life controls everything human from the generic level of bio-psychic instincts. The root-potential of the human organism is being cultivated in common and made to blossom out by men who likewise are one in the cultivation of the earth. Every member of the tribe has an inalienable right to his share in it, and whatever power he uses, he uses it only as a *functional entity,* as one cell in a communal organism. But when the organic unanimity of the tribe breaks down, and the process of individualization through strife, lust and acquisitiveness becomes universal, then, individualized men come to claim the wealth and power developed by communal cultivation and civilization as their own—whenever they can get hold of some

portion of this wealth and power. The concept of "individual property" spreads over all sense of possession and all forms of power,
all agencies for the release of this power from nature.

This "antithetical" approach to power cannot endure forever.
As releases of power become ever more complex and large-scale
operations, requiring collective skill and permanent cooperation
among the men who engineer the process of release; as the energies
released become increasingly intense and destructive (at least in
potentiality), the need for social preservation compels individualistic men who cling to their absolute right of private ownership to
relinquish (gradually, or violently) at least a part of their possessions and power to the whole community. Thus the dualism of
private and public ownership is established, as a matter of fact
and as a matter of compulsive *need*. It remains to philosophers and
to planners of the future society to interpret, codify and generalize
the inevitable process, so that out of it a new consciousness of per-
sonality-to-society relationship becomes sufficiently definite and
generally accepted to become a foundation for this new society—
a typical *weltanschauung* (life-orientation).

The social types of the "manager" and the "engineer" have
emerged out of the need for specialized individuals able to handle
the complex mechanisms for release of power devised during the
last hundred years and to organize the infinitely varied groupings
of operations and of human beings required in modern production
—or modern destruction. There are engineers and managers of all
types, working with extremely varied kinds of substances, engines,
factories and distributing processes. Some operate on purely material substances, others deal with group-psychology and the minds
of men. Some run productive plants, others the distributing of
news, still others huge operations such as the Normandy invasion.
Characteristic of all these managerial activities in modern society
is the complexity of factors to be organized into an operative whole,

and the need for a technical mastery of planning at the intellectual organizational level. Time and space factors must be controlled in a way completely unknown in earlier ages, and cold objectivity is required in the handling of matters in which the personal human equation should be eliminated as far as possible because of the unpredictability involved in any individual case. Managerial planning is essentially statistical. It deals with averages, with collectivities. And it tends to depersonalize and mechanize the human being.

It is for this reason that, if the society of tomorrow is not to become geared to a de-humanized type of productivity efficiently managed by ruthless managers and technicians, it is absolutely necessary to establish *as a basic fact of the harmonic society* the polar dualism of private and public life, of individually usable power and of power whose use is determined by collective purpose. It is equally necessary so to imbue the managers of tomorrow (and of today, if possible!) with the new ideal of service in conscious participation and with the concrete social expression of the "transpersonal way", that they dedicate their minds and wills as co-creators of the necessary agencies for the actual incorporation of Man.

In other words, using as a foundation the *fact* that today the manager-technician type of human being is becoming the most characteristic (and probably soon the most dominant) type of social being, the *ideal* of the server should be established in every possible way, so as to give a constructive meaning, direction and spiritual character to this type. Just as the warrior type of man in the early Middle Ages became, as the feudal lord, the dominant social type and had to be "spiritualized" into the Knight fighting a "holy war" against infidels and also against his own passions—so, today the fast-spreading manager-technician type has to be given an ideal meaning and direction, if it is not to control tyrannically the future society. And the kind of mentality characteristic of the type has to be integrated within a larger framework of human values and personality development, in which it is only an organic part and not a hypertrophied, all-absorbing and eventually health-destroying function.

If the new society is to be a harmonic society, it must be able to "assimilate" the manager type and the technician's mentality—or else it will become absorbed and tyrannized by them. Society can only assimilate this manager type by generalizing its meaning, by meeting its challenges, by placing it where it can belong to the whole of society as an organic function, by re-orienting it in terms of all-human purpose and balancing it by stressing its polar opposite in the total life of man. The manager function becomes generalized if our present generation succeeds in establishing the principle that *every man and woman* should be a manager of all those powers and faculties which, being collective in their social origin, can only constitute a public trust given to the individual. As all wealth which was produced, or which can be increased, by collective social activities comes to be regarded as wealth for the management of which the individual holding it is responsible to society, half of the life of *all* human beings becomes interpretable in terms of management. The other half is given to the personal use of one's truly individual and private possessions, over which the individual has an absolute right of ownership.

Thus the old injunction of Christ in a new form: "*Manage* for society these possessions that the collective work of society has produced or increased; but *individualize* in your self, through the fullest and most significant use possible, the substance of your own being with which life and God have endowed you". The true server is the man who, because as an individual person he is able to cultivate fully within himself his own spiritual "seed" or Self (that which in him is "Man" or divine Sonship), is always ready to participate consciously and unreservedly in the work of society as manager of his share of social wealth and vitality.

From a negative and wasteful bureaucracy
to a positive and creative Civil Service

It is not enough to differentiate the sphere of management of social-collective power (or wealth) from that of private use of powers for which the individual is responsible only to life or God. The next step is to establish the social and psychological conditions necessary to make this management fully efficient, vital, bold and creative of new values.

It is commonly believed today that management by men who are working as "civil servants" for society and for the state is *inevitably* tainted by the evils of bureaucracy; by inefficiency, slothfulness, lack of imagination, red tape and unwillingness to assume personal responsibiltiy. That such is mostly the case today is undeniable, even in countries where the accepted emphasis is upon collectivism and state-socialism. That this is an inevitable fact, due to some special quirk of "human nature", seems to be a senseless assertion based on lack of historical perspective and psychological understanding.

In a historical society in which individual differentation through strife, rebellion and pain is the evolutionary law, it is obvious that any type of activity which does not feature this competitive and acquisitive goal, and which establishes a life-long reposeful heaven from which one may hardly ever fall into the hell of social strife and job hunting, is bound to attract human beings who, either are still unborn as individuals, or (having been hurt and defeated before) seek social peace and security at all cost, or accept a job which needs no special concentration or self-mobilization in order to pursue some hobby or some financially unproductive occupation in their spare time. The special security of the civil service job must therefore be kept by every possible means, especially by avoiding any potentially dangerous display of initiative, by playing politics and by withdrawing behind the impersonal anonymity of formulas, official documents, standardization and red tape.

Beside this, it is also obvious that most individuals who today come from small towns, and even more (for instance, in Russia) from peasants' villages, are congenitally and mentally unprepared to participate, with conscious responsibility and creative initiative, in a vast social organization whose scope, purpose and techniques are utterly beyond their mental power fully and vitally to encompass and experience. Even the leaders in such vast organizations—whether under private or state control—are often able to get only an intellectually schematic grasp of its intricate mechanisms. This grasp, in order to be kept operative, has to be constantly fortified and concretized by graphs, charts and classifications; which in turn are translated into forms, circulars, memory-aides, etc., standardizing and depersonalizing most productive operations into set departmentalized procedures. And where the managing power of the whole organization is itself impersonal and depending upon fluctuating parliamentary controls and public opinion—and also answerable to constant press criticism and influenced by unofficial pressure-groups—the evils of bureaux and of dispersion of authority necessarily increase. They are not, however, inherent in state-organization and national "civil service," but rather in *any* institution whose scope is such that it makes departmentalization and hierarchic procedures necessary—whether the institution is controlled by private owners, or a group of state-managers, or a religious hierarchy operating under "spiritual" (and also economic!) sanctions.

Nevertheless humanity has reached a point in its evolution when global organization is necessary, in view of the character of the productive powers mankind now uses and of the requirements of global all-human interchange. We must have large-scale organization. We must have managers and a vast civil service—and a hierarchy of operative levels and managerial functions. We must have a host of highly specialized technicians. Or else we must forego all that our modern civilization has brought forth—a defeatist and unacceptable solution. What then is the valid and constructive solution? *We must develop a new type of human beings endowed with new mental and spiritual powers, with a new psychology.* We must *educate* every man and woman to fulfill his and her trust and responsibility to society as a "manager," as one trained to handle the powers produced by the vastly complex psychological and economic interchanges of our global society, as well as by our intricate machines. We must deliberately and consciously set our generation to the great task of training its men and women and their children so that they may be ready to assume their shares of creative responsibility, as conscious and mature participants in the global ritual of the new society—*as servers, consecrated to the two-fold purpose of such a harmonic society.*

Our schools and colleges are utterly inadequate and unprepared in providing such an education for service and self-consecration to managerial tasks. They train the intellect (mostly the powers of memory!) so that it can comprehend and solve, with the aid of tables and references, technical problems. They hardly do anything else. They fail particularly to develop in students any constructive personal and social psychology, any sound and creative approach to adult life and to the necessary problems arising from cooperation in terms of free personal exchange of values, emotional or mental. They still emphasize the competitive spirit and obsolete differences of nation, class, color and religion—especially in all extra-curricular activities (fraternities, sports, church-services, etc.). Because they do not *start* from the common foundation upon which everything human has ever been built—man's common humanity, as we defined it in our third chapter—, because they still hold to the fairy-tale myth that all society begins with single individuals who deliberately form families, tribes, nations, etc., they cannot give any sensible and constructive meaning to a society which can only exist harmoniously on the conscious interplay between the whole and the individual, and *on the creative responsibility of both to each other.*

The schools and colleges are not alone in having to be blamed for modern man's inability to serve society in complete self-consecration to an all-human purpose, while developing to the full his individual personality. The general attitude of men and women— and especially of our legislators—toward the discharge of public responsibilities and the use, misuse and abuse of collective social power is incredibly unsound, obsolete and destructive of efficiency. A person committing an injury to an individual or to his property is considered a dangerous criminal; but a policeman, an army leader or any civil servant whose inefficiency, misuse of public trust, or abuse of social power and official authority is proven usually meets only discharge from office or demotion, reprimand or very slight penalty.

This fact is the foundation of most bureaucratic evils and most types of public mis-administration. Our democratic society is still so completely obsessed by the rights of the individual and the sanctity of private ownership, and so blind to the responsibility of the individual to the social whole, that any harm to the individual is a heinous "crime," but harm to society by a person entrusted by society with the management of social power and the use of official authority is merely, in most cases, a "negligence." A policeman may abuse the power of his office in the most flagrant manner, and merely find himself discharged. A general may, through negligence or inefficiency, lead thousands to slaughter, and is, at the worst, brought back home to a comfortable pension. Are such occurrences not outrageous and destructive of any efficiency in public management? When will modern society come to recognize that indubitably proven inefficiency in discharging a public function, leading to waste of social power in any form, is a crime nearly as great as taking the life of an individual; that the misuse of collective power delegated to an individual by virtue of his office is the worst crime of all, for it attacks the very foundation of that social organism in which *all* individuals participate?

Any "officer of the law," who uses his social power and official prestige to intimidate or coerce in any way any person, perpetrates an offense worse than the rape or kidnapping of an individual by another private individual. Moreover any "civil servant" who fails to take the necessary initiative to meet an emergency in his own field of responsibility commits also a social offense. He injures society by failing to act when it was his responsibility to act. He should, at the very least, be sent back to many months of further training, *both psychological and technical*. He is not "guilty" as an individual person, but as a manager of social power. As an individual he has the right to full education and to the full opportunity of proving his worth; but as a manager of social power and as a servant of society he has the responsibility to perform effectively the work which he has accepted—and only the right to learn further and try again, if his failure does not reveal complete lack of ability in the field he selected.

These are only a very few of a multitude of examples which could be given to show what education for management and a new sense of public service to humanity would concretely mean. The essential point is that our attitude to management and service *must* be changed utterly if we can ever hope to meet the problems and challenges of modern productivity and large-scale organization in all conceivable fields. A new attitude to all social activities and responsibilities is indeed absolutely needed if the new society is to operate harmonically and creatively, on the double basis of total productivity and individual responsibility. And at the very root of this new attitude there must be a new psychology—a new understanding of the human person.

This does not mean giving up the spiritual principles which the great spiritual leaders of humanity exemplified in their lives and their *original* teachings. This does not mean, particularly, to abandon the fundamental attitude of the Christ toward the individual. It means to establish on a new and harmonic basis the *relationship* of this individual to a completely transformed society—his participation in, and his service to, a society in which for the first time in history the harmonic principle of "plenitude" (personal-spiritual as well as material-economic) can and must replace the law of scarcity and individual differentiation through generalized strife, exclusivism and intolerance.

We should indeed retain the spirit of Christ and vivify by it our private search for God and our intimate relationship with our "companions." What is to be built, however, is a new public sense of responsibility to society, a new sense of service and dedication, a new understanding of the sacred nature of any public trust to an individual; not merely as a religious ideal usually negated by actual social practices, but as a practical fact of the life of social service and management—the life in which both man and woman have now to participate, because it is only out of a conscious and purposeful interchange of polarities that there can be fullness of being (in personality) and steady productivity (in society).

Man and Woman, as "Co-Servers"

At the biological level of productivity and bearing forth, man and woman operate as husand and wife, as father and mother. At the strictly social and ideological level of conscious and individualized productivity, the polar relationship of the man and woman servers manifests in new ways. The rhythm, focalization and scope of this productive relationship are no longer determined by sexual structures and by the fecundative act; they are conditioned essentially by the polarities inherent in all social and cultural manifestations.

We defined society as an "associative field"—we might almost say an "electro-magnetic field"—in which human activities (physical, psychic and mental) are organized and structured by collective ideals and lines of forces, as loose iron filings are drawn into patterns within a magnetic field. We speak of "lines of forces," or of *idées-forces*: and this means that two factors are recognizable. There is structure (lines, ideas or images) and there is force or current. Indeed the trinity of energy, form and substance—demonstrated through a fourth term, activity—is a universal fact. This fact is expressed in terms of social organization, in reverse order, as: the collective need for a new product or a new type of organization (and for wages), the inventive and organizing vision which plans the production, and the power that precipitates the plan into concrete operation. The fourth term is the work of production itself, the activity of the workmen and of everyone intent upon satisfying the collective needs.

Today, for instance, the desperate human need is for a world-organization that will establish a permanent state of peace. The United Nations constitute an answer—albeit a tentative and imperfect one— to that need. It was planned by the Big Three and their aids, particularly it seems by Franklin D. Roosevelt. It was projected into actual being ("managed") by the State Departments of the nations who organized and led the San Francisco Conference; and lastly it started its operations. In this case, as in the case of any kind of factory production, there are those who conceive the plan of the production (who make, or accept, the blue-prints and who set general policies) and those who put the plan into actual operation.

Thus two basic functions: the pattern-making or policy-making function, and the managerial or technique-applying function. The first is characteristic of the man-polarity in social activity; the second, of the woman-polarity—when woman will assume her full share of responsibility at the social non-biological level of productivity. Typically or symbolically speaking, man is the architect; woman, the contractor. Man is the executive; woman, the administrator. Man deals primarily with concepts, ideas and directives or distant goals; woman, with human relationships and the handling of people in the immediate fulfillment of everyday tasks. Man tends by nature to deal with the abstract and the general; woman, with the concrete and the particular. Man thinks in terms of "form," where woman deals normally with "body." The mind of man functions essentially in a realm of *ideas;* while woman's nature makes her at home in the world of *energy*—and both together, therefore, can release into effective social operation creative *idées-forces,* concepts charged with vital power, ideological "seed" that will grow into actual, concrete organizations of social substance and activity.

In our modern Western civilization woman's most characteristic and most frequent participation in the complex ritual of social production and distribution is, at present, as secretary and sales-woman. In both functions, she is essentially the contact-point between the business-man who produces goods, and the public who buys them or the various persons who seek to influence the producer. She deals therefore with human relationships and associative energies. The secretary of a big executive distributes the daily work and appointments, handles correspondence, files and records; thus, she focuses the executive's attention upon old procedures and the *new needs* of customers, employees and associates. Through her, the demands of the outer world of human beings reach the executive, who answers them by setting new policies and goals. She clarifies the need of society to the man who can fill that need; and, in this, she fulfills woman's essential nature which, as we wrote in a previous chapter, is to focus the need of today and to condition the release of a creative spiritual solution by her expectancy and her faith in progressive tomorrows. The quality of woman's expectancy determines the character of the creative release of spirit through the man she loves. Likewise, many a big executive finds his policies subtly, but none the less effectively, determined (or at least conditioned) by the manner in which the many problems and people he must deal with are screened and presented to him by his trusted secretary. And this applies preeminently to our national Executive and his Secretaries or Administrators!

The relationship of the business man to his secretary has been in recent years the subject of countless novels, dramas and short stories in which the more ludicrous or sexual-emotional factors were given, in most cases, the main importance. But, whenever such a widespread social type of personal involvements is noticeable, it can usually be considered as the manifestation of an underlying evolutionary trend breaking at the surface of social behavior, whether in dramatic waves or in humorous ripples of foam. This deeper trend in human relationship is the eagerness, in the more spiritually or socially developed men and women, to unite their productive energies at a new and more conscious level of social operation, and above all to come together within the set-up of a common work, rather than in terms of the traditional patterns created by humanity to foster and protect instinctual biological ends.

Women, in the past, have worked with men under various conditions; but in practically all cases that work has been associated with the bio-cultural idea of the "home." Working in the fields, or in a small merchandise store, meant still working in an extended home or family-property; and the purpose of the work was to build, sustain and develop the "family." The family was the productive unit; it was also an enveloping matrix. Within the womb-like and semi-tribal collective personality of the family and its material field of possessions, woman worked — not in company with man, as much as "in compulsive instinctual conjunction" with man.

Family-work is bound up with ownership—"my" home, "my" children, "my" business—; and this ownership is strictly private, at least since the disintegration of aristocratic traditions according to which a family was a social-political entity and the heads of it were responsible for the welfare of many slaves, servants or related people. Neither husband nor wife have to render accounts to society for the use they make of such a private field of bio-cultural productivity. This concept of ownership without public responsibility is gradually being challenged today; society has a voice in the children's education, private business operations are subjected to regulations, etc. But the individualistic concept of the bourgeois family as a strictly private possessive unit is still implanted in mass-psychology—even though modern industrialism and the tempo of business, frequent divorces and the encouragement of sheer self-assertiveness in children, have tended to make such a concept, if not obsolete, at least of relative and questionable value.

Public work, on the other hand, when jointly performed by men and women, gives an entirely new character to this joint performance. In this case, the man and woman do not work in terms of biological or proprietary instinct. They are co-workers whose activities are conditioned or determined by a social structure regulating factors of production which they either do not own, or which they own *only in trust* for society as a whole. They are, at least potentially, "Companions" participating consciously and as individual personalities in a super-personal group-purpose. Their cooperative work is oriented to such a purpose, in the determination of which they should freely participate. It is work in terms of efficient management, instead of proprietary instinct.

This ideal is obviously not realized today; most people neither understand or accept it, because it opposes their rootedness in biological and tribal instinctiveness. Nevertheless it is obviously the new evolutionary goal for humanity; a goal made inescapable by the pressure of modern facts of production and distribution, of individual and group psychology, of science and technology. It is the as yet but dimly understood drive toward such a goal of cooperative companionship in terms of management of public values or wealth, which seeks to bring about a new relationship between men and women associated in such a type of work.

At first, public work for women has meant freedom from biological and house-keeping tasks, freedom from traditional fields of near-servitude, from instinctual compulsions, social prejudices and enforced ignorance. This was the antithesis to the old thesis. The next step to be taken is the synthesis: Woman, in the fullness of her characteristic nature, serving, in companionship with man, the purpose of a social group, toward the goal of total productivity and in creative freedom of mature personality. By cooperating with others within a public organization, woman can transmute her ancient proprietary instinct into consecrated service. The manager-secretary relationship can assimilate this new sense of service, in both the man and the woman; and it must repolarize its un-creative and "impersonal" character (or its superficially personal and sexual overtones) into a consciously personalized cooperation consecrated to the fullest possible productivity.

There cannot be full productivity except on the basis of conscious and consecrated personality. The new productive man-woman relationship has to integrate the personal and impersonal factors found in the fact of the togetherness in work of a man and a woman, whether in an office or anywhere where work is done in terms of a consciously understood social goal. It must be personalized within a super-personal frame of reference—thus, it must become a transpersonal productive relationship. It cannot admit a sense of instinctive possessiveness or an emphasis upon proprietary rights—and yet it can be, it must be a relationship energized by, and fulfilled in, the creative warmth of personality; a relationship between two servers who are also companions, co-participants in the ritual of the "work of the world."

Indeed the transpersonal way is, at every level and in every realm of human activity, a practical way which determines a new quality of human productivity as well as a new method of personality-unfoldment leading to psychological maturity. It is so because wherever there is human life and consciously individualized activity one can always distinguish two polarities between which flows constantly a current of productive interchange—or destructive interchange, if hate, jealousy or envy supersede love or the companionship of joint consecration to a collective work. This mutual interpenetration between man and woman must be given today a new meaning in the realm of social and business activity—or else, it indeed turns destructive and manifests as subtle or overt social enmity between the women and men of the community, or at least as competition for jobs (regardless of the appropriateness of such jobs for women). Constructively understood, and vivified or spiritualized by the transpersonal ideal of joint and consecrated service, the relationship of man and woman at the concrete social level of everyday work can renew the very fabric of society.

More than anything else perhaps it could serve the purpose— the most important and critical purpose—of giving a more idealistic and spiritual direction to the inevitable emergence of a class of managers-technicians who may indeed become the real rulers of our future global society in the name of total productivity and efficiency. And we should not forget that there are managers of mass-psychology as well as of factories; that there are technicians who master mass-propaganda and the ways of making psychic fears and religious superstitions serve the selfish purposes of groups intent on keeping their old social privileges or increasing their power over society!

Women in the days of the Crusades were largely influential in transforming the feudal warriors and robber-barons into knights and consecrated servants of God and of the oppressed people; women today can exert their influence powerfully in helping the various types of managers of our society to become members of a consecrated "Civil Service" which also can set aright many present day injustices and forms of social and business oppression. They can do so as secretaries for, and co-workers with these managers and technicians who might be only too ready to sacrifice the rights of individuals on the altar of productive efficiency. It is the woman's task to stand for "right human relations" in all spheres of social activities, of management of power and wealth; to stand for the individual person against the machine; to tread with the men the transpersonal way; and so to meet men in the public life of work, as well as, and even more perhaps than, in the private life of the home, that the woman's expectancy and faith may become a powerful determinant in the conversion of these managers of our intellectualized and depersonalized society to the concrete and practical religion of Man, to the service of the divine purpose for humanity.

We indeed need, in the world of ever bigger Big Business and of totalitarian states ruthlessly controlling production through scientific and technique-haunted managers, a new type of "chivalry" adapted to our modern mentality. We need a new sense of dedication of the managerial and technical mind to an all-human purpose. We need a crusade against all that depersonalizes and mechanizes human beings and human lives, whether in "communistic" or in "democratic" countries. The process of de-humanizing men was begun a century ago mostly in the Anglo-American countries. We should thus be the first ones to take the lead in this crusade.

The crusade, however, should begin at the level of the man-woman relationship; where men and women work together; where they should learn to *serve* together, as companions in the great Company of Man, as conscious and mature participants in the performances of a harmonized humanity determined to usher in the era of plenitude, of total productivity by all and for all—a total productivity engineered by men and women self-determined and free, but dedicated to the whole, radiant in the purpose of the whole.

THE ROAD TO GLOBAL HARMONY

There is only one world, one globe for men to dwell upon; but every point on this globe has its antipode. To ignore this fact is naive. Many people are very naive in this hemisphere. One wonders if they really believe we live on a globe; and if they would not much rather think that the earth is flat, and *their* hemisphere—of course—the whole of this flat earth. Unity, yes; but *through* the harmonization and integration of two polarities. To fail to admit that these polarities exist is to dream oneself out of concrete existence *via* the atomic bomb; whoever uses it first.

During the centuries of our Western civilization dominated by the Hebraized Christianity of St. Paul and the transcendentalism of a perhaps misunderstood Platonic philosophy, European thinkers (and their American relatives), when confronted with the problem of duality, have almost exclusively considered it to refer to the dualism of heaven and earth, of spirit and matter, and (as they understood it) of good and evil. Their attitude has been based primarily on a "either-or" concept of exclusivism. Anything was either black or white, constructive or destructive, of God or of the Devil—true or false. Today, most people, having absorbed implicitly such a traditional type of thinking, consider that a people or nation is democratic (good) or un-democratic (bad), free or oppressed, progressive or regressive. It seems rarely to occur to the average person that democracy, freedom and progress in a nation are always a matter of "more-or-less," and never a matter of "either-or." Still more important, however, is the fact that it is rare to find people who believe that every productive realization and every creative activity, requires the correlation and cooperation of two polarized efforts— of two complementary (therefore opposite) points of view and angles of approach. Thus, for instance, of man and woman.

169

This creative kind of polar opposition must not be confused however with the one existing between good and evil, and usually symbolized by black and white. A black object is one which absorbs all light and reflects or redistributes none at all to its surroundings. Thus blackness or evil characterizes a state of total selfishness and greed for light. Anyone who, as a matter of set policy, seeks to grab all power for himself alone and gives nothing in return to society, is "black." The evil being is not the one deprived of light, but the one who gives out no light at all. Day is not "good" and night "evil." There can be real evil only where there is light and power in abundance. Evil is a type of response to light and power in which the ego gluttonously monopolizes the released energy and illumination, leaving all other men in a state of deprivation and spiritual hunger.

It is for this reason that social evil reaches its peak whenever a sudden increase of power and wealth is released and made available to an individual person or a nation. Most illnesses are the results of congestion: the blood supply becomes hoarded by an organ. Likewise, when a class of people cling avidly, for their own selfish use and aggrandizement, to the power which the collectivity has entrusted to them in an emergency such as war, or when an enormous rise in social productivity after new discoveries mobilizes and makes available abnormally large amounts of energy, and the privileged ruling class rushes in to corner this new supply—then, a society becomes "black" with greed and hoarded wealth or power.

Cases to the point are quite obvious. The rise of England as a world-power, after her navy obtained control of the vast amount of gold mined by the Spanish conquerors and being transported to Spain, is an illustration. The rise of the United States and of its millionaire class of Big Business adventures since the Industrial Revolution, the conquest of the West and the discovery of gold in the late forties, is another instance. The possibility that Russian militarists and ambitious men might use the tremendous increase in world-power and prestige of their nation, following the defeat of Germany, as a means to establish control over an expanding Soviet Society is likewise a crucial factor in the present world-situation. But the very same possibility confronts us in America, with the military and Big Business seeking to control the new atomic power and the expanded American economy. The rise of a class of black market operators, when inflation mobilizes and releases paper-money wealth, is likewise a typical manifestation of social evil.

Evil spares no man and no nation. The most that can be said is that a man and a nation can become at times focal points for the operation of this tendency toward greed. The tendency is potentiality inherent in humanity, simply because man is by nature destined to become a manager of power. The dualism of good and evil as we know it today refers thus to man's attitude toward the use of power and it becomes sharpened in its effect whenever a great increase of available energy and wealth (spiritual as well as material) makes the problem of *how* and *what-for* to use power a vividly defined issue—a "black and white" issue.

When we spoke of global polarities in the performance of productive work by an integrated humanity we referred, however, to an entirely different type of dualism—the organic polarization of healthy bodies, and not the contrast between health (good) and disease (evil). Global polarities become a fact the moment the surface of the earth is seen as, and actually becomes, the habitat of an integrated society including all men and excluding none from its opportunities. These polarities are necessary for the functioning of this "One World" of which imaginative men dream, but which they often fail to understand in its inevitable *organic* implications. In true American fashion many liberals have become enthused and eloquent about the *ideal* of this one world, while failing to grasp the *concrete realities* inevitably developing from the establishment in fact of a productively functioning global society.

To function productively requires polarization. A productive global society implies a polarized society operating throughout an organically differentiated field of production, the earth-surface. We have to think, not of the world as a unity, but of the world as an organic whole, upholding and sustaining an organic humanity. And as interplanetary contacts are not of the immediate future, and as we do not even know whether or not there are other humanities on neighboring planets, we have to consider our earth-globe as the entire field for production; which means, as a closed bi-polar field.

There are regions and peoples on earth that are, by virtue of their geographical positions and of their racial-cultural temperaments, particularly destined to assume polar functions in the global economy (material and psycho-spiritual) of the immediate future. And it is only as these peoples and their leaders recognize this polar inter-relationship as a basic fact of geography, history, religion, culture and commerce, that the foundation for an integrated humanity can be established. Recognizing this polar inter-relatedness and willing to assume the responsibilities derived from it, these peoples will, as a result, enter upon the road of *harmony in mutuality* within the structure of global planning.

We are speaking here, in terms of immediate political realities, of the United States of America and of the Union of Socialist Soviet Republics; but we actually mean far more, and are reaching far deeper, than politics and present-day nations. We are speaking of the two great continental masses of the earth-surface, and of their peoples. We are referring to the *function* which each *must* sooner or later play in the spiritual-material economy of an integrated global humanity. We are referring to it, not in terms of the old-type of English and German "geopolitics," from MacKinder to Haushofer and his Munich School, but in terms of harmonious and organic function in a new society vivified by a spirit of productive world-companionship among nations that experience themselves as participants in a global all-human social whole, consecrated to Man.

And we are speaking here in very concrete and tangible terms; not of ideals, but of factual necessities, which have indeed a life-or-death urgency in our atomic Age.

Elements of Global Morphology

Let us look at the earth-globe. We should have learned to see it as a globe pivoting around the polar axis; its continental masses of land and oceans dotted with islands, big and small, spreading over its surface in characteristic shapes. Here mankind lives. Within this global field men produce and strive to reach harmony within themselves and with one another—strive, alas, so far most unsuccessfully as a rule. How can they hope to reach harmony as men, if they do not understand the harmony that chords all lands and seas as a dynamic whole, as an integral field of operation? The earth-surface is a whole, and it is dynamic in as much as it is constantly in motion and in a state of morphological change. The earth whirls in space in a complex combination of motions which constantly modify the "geomorphic" and geostatic equilibrium of its lands, seas and air-currents. Mountains and continents rise and fall. Ice ages come in waves. There may be even greater changes in the polarization and axial inclination of our globe as a whole, whence vast cataclysms that imprint deep-seated remembrances in the collective unconscious of all civilizations.

The earth may not be strictly speaking "alive"; but it is the matrix —or matricial "field"—from which all living organisms emerge and within which they operate in unity or diversity, as material organisms and as participants in a cosmic-planetary drama of evolution. Most living organisms remain unconscious of this participation, live and die in a, to them, meaningless sequence. A few human beings at all times reach full and direct consciousness of this great evolution; give to their less aware comrades visions and symbols to foreshadow what the latter in turn may come to experience;

and, passing on, remain as indivisible units of consciousness and power within the great oneness of Man.

From the thin layers of this earth-surface, all life springs forth. Surely, if we can only visualize and understand our global world as a whole of organically (or quasi-organically) inter-related parts and functions, we may end by sensing and perhaps clearly understanding what each of these continental and oceanic parts represents in the economy of the whole. What we need is a sense of *gestalt*—that is, of integral form—and of symbolic values; to which the records of history (and even of persistent world-wide tradition) should add much meaning, if they too are understood in terms of "wholes of time," i.e. of cycles. We need a new approach to geography and to the geographical basis of history and civilization; we need, both, an integrative approach and an engineer's approach—thus we need branches of knowledge which we have called respectively "geomorphics" and "geotechnics."

Our planet is a whole; human civilization is a whole. In the Age of plenitude, of which we speak throughout this book, creative fulfillment can only come to man as these wholes are taken as foundations for living, feeling and thinking. The now obsolete European geopolitics was not based on such a goal of total human fulfillment and productivity. It was only a realistic foundation for the "struggle for power" which is the essence of politics, a broad and intelligent foundation for the effective domination by one or more nations and classes of the energies available on this globe. American Technocracy, while less obvious in its purpose, ultimately would reach toward a similar goal under a Howard Scott type of engineer-controller. Geopolitics deals with states, with the conquering urges of nations which "must be educated up from smaller to larger space conceptions," or decay as the "result of a declining space conception" (Frederich Ratzel).

In the Age of global plenitude which we envision *politics would be superseded by management.* States would become managerial organizations concerned only with the planning and maintaining of full production. The old legalistic structure of the state, which is the legacy of the Roman world and which has only the value of an expedient, would operate in terms of management of energy. *There is no meaning in "law" except in the realm of management of power; every other field of human activity should operate under the principle of "harmony in mutuality."*

We italicized the above statements because they are fundamental, and we shall develop them further elsewhere. What we call "geotechnics" is the science of management of the total resources of the earth as an all-inclusive field of operation. And by "geomorphics" we mean the understanding of the structure of this field, not primarily in terms of the amount of materials, energy and human beings available for production on each and all lands or seas, but rather in terms of the geomorphic structure and shape of continents and oceans. These global structures, after all, condition climates and population, migrations and the course of civilization. They are as significant to anyone attempting to understand the past, present and future of humanity as a whole, as the study of the shape of a person's body and features is to the endocrinologist and psychologist (or even criminologist) whose business it is to understand the temperament, character and behavior of men. We might thus speak of geomorphics as a kind of "geognomy" similar in intent to physiognomy; a modern and "scientific" version of the latter having been provided by Dr. Sheldon's studies in *The Varieties of Human Physique* (Harper, 1940) and his classification of human bodies and temperaments into viscerotonic, somatotonic, and cerebrotonic.

We can only briefly suggest here the possibilities of this new field of geomorphic study, but a typical instance can be pointed out which will lead us to the main point of this chapter. This instance is the remarkable morphologic similarity between Asia and Europe. Both Asia and Europe have three southward peninsulas. Indo-China, India and Arabia match respectively Greece, Italy and

Spain. Ceylon is the structural equivalent of Sicily; Indonesia, of Crete and the Greek archipelago down to Rhodes (which is, in a very general sense, a miniature Australia).

If we look at the continental mainland, we find Tibet (and the adjacent mountain ranges of China) matching Switzerland and Bohemia. The Mongolian and Siberian plains correspond to Germany and Poland. China in the East is like European Russia; while in the West, central France stands for Persia, with Brittany shaped much like Asia Minor, and the French Atlantic coast below Brittany, like Syria and Palestine—the Gironde and Dordogne valleys with their prehistoric cultures paralleling that of the Tigris and Euphrates.

Such correspondences might seem mere chance figurations were it not that there is a startling parallelism between the characteristics of the cultures which have developed in these corresponding geographical structures. Indo-China with her highly developed art and music, and Java with her rich culture, remind one forcibly of Greece and the earlier Cretan civilizations. India has been the center of religious doctrines for Asia, just as Italy has been for Europe. The ancient city of Nasik, sacred to Rama, stands (near Bombay) where Rome is in Italy; Benares, where Florence grew. Curiously enough the Arabs settled in Spain (Arabia's structural equivalent in Europe), and both Arabia and Spain are rugged lands, angular shaped, with fanatic, intense, proud populations. As significant are the historical-cultural correspondences between the nations which grew respectively in Persia and in France (Zoroastrian civilization matching the old Celtic culture), in Mongolia and in Germany (military and mystical peoples avid for space-conquest in an inorganic sense), in China and Russia (lands of the "good earth" and of robust peasantry long controlled by a small aristocracy).

The general picture presented by the relationship of Europe to Asia is that of miniature to full-sized original. Europe is not unlike the budding protuberance on a navel orange, which is a small

replica of the orange itself. It appears thus as a specialized reproduction of the vast Motherland for a particular evolutionary purpose. In another sense, of real historical-cultural validity, we might
say that Europe is to Asia as the conscious and intellectual part of
man's total psyche is to the vast collective unconscious. The conscious is a differentiated organ of the unconscious, in the sense that
the brain and the cerebrospinal nervous system constitute differentiated organs of the total human organism. Religion is the progeny
of the collective unconscious (Asia); science, that of the rational
conscious (Europe)

In such a parallelism differences are as significant as similarities.
We spoke of Italy and India, Switzerland and Tibet as occupying
similar places in the two geomorphic structures. But we should
notice at once the fact that the Alps describe a convex arc of
mountains above the Northern Italian plains, while the Himalayas
describe a concave arc over the plains of Northern India. If we consider the two mountainous masses of Switzerland and Tibet as the
"geo-spiritual" centers of their respective continents, we get the
idea of the European center radiating outward, while the Asiatic
center is focused inward; and we see how well this describes the
difference between the European and Asiatic types of spirituality.

Another way of looking at the Eurasian land-mass is to see it
as one shape extending from 10° longitude west (West Ireland) to
170° longitude west (Eastern tip of Siberia). Dividing into two
this span of 200 degrees of longitude, we find longitude 90° east
as the pivotal meridian; and it passes through Calcutta, Tibet, near
Lhassa and near the highest mountain of the globe, just west of
the Gobi Desert and the Mongolian People's Republic, through a
most important part of Siberia (Sibirsk region) and along the great
Ienisei river which may become a great trade-route in the future.
Around the pivot of this 90° east meridian we might see soon the
total population of the Eurasian world almost evenly divided; even
now the combined population of India, Persia and the U.S.S.R.

balance approximately that of China, Japan, Indo-China and Indo-nesia. And there is a general similarity of position between the Scandinavian peninsula and Kamchatka, the British Isles and Japan —the correlation between the last two island-groups being particularly significant in terms of world-history and racial background.

The main point we wish to make here, however, is the polar relationship between, on one hand, the big land mass constituted by Europe, Asia and Africa (or "Eurasiafrica"), and on the other, the Americas. This relationship provides the logical foundation for the future global society. It establishes the great geomorphic dualism of human civilization. Just as the North and South Polar regions are complementary in that the former is an apparently empty circle of water, while the latter is a quasi-circular land-mass; so the two basic continental structures of the earth, America and Eurasiafrica, have shapes whose characteristics complement and polarize each other.

The Americas can be reduced in shape to two southward pointing triangles—a symbol of "descent" of spirit and "masculine" activity—; while Eurasiafrica is a sprawling "feminine" shape, with Europe as a highly differentiated miniature form of the great mother of races and religions, Asia. Some geologists have claimed that at one time the two continental masses were united, then broke away very slowly (over many tens of thousands of years)—the line of fission being now the Atlantic ocean. The western contour of Europe-Africa and the eastern shores of the Americas suggest broadly such a possibility—if the western bulge of Africa is made to fit into the depression of the Gulf of Mexico and the southern coast of the United States.

We are inclined to believe that the mythical Atlantis might have been, rather than a now sunken continent, this whole continental mass *before it broke in two;* in other words, the earth's continents in a condition of undivided unity—whereas now they constitute essentially two polarized masses. This would be significant—

if it could be proven true—in that it would correlate with the myth-ological reference to an Atlantean humanity, at first pure and sin-less, *then dividing into two camps* as a result of the abuse and mis-use of sexual powers.

However this may be, the fact is that today man's global field of operation is typically bi-polar. At the center of the two land-masses we find, in Eurasiafrica, the Mediterranean Sea and, in the Americas, the Gulf of Mexico. The former has been a focal point for Eurasiafrican culture; the latter has also been, and presumably will even more become, a focus for the Pan-American culture which, after a number of centuries (and perhaps even millennia) will grad-ually be established, we may well presume, as an entirely new human expression. Today "American" civilization, North and South, is fundamentally an outgrowth of European impulses and ideologies; and we believe it is merely a matrix into which new spiritual seeds have been and are being sown, which will take a very long time to mature, through many crises and probable obscurations. It seems likely that the first typical developments in truly American culture will come from the lands surrounding the Gulf of Mexico—Mexico itself being a probable focus, as it also was in the time of the May-ans, and perhaps long before.

All of which may be called "speculations", and must remain so until a new understanding of planetary cycles of geological and anthropological development is reached. What is factual and very concrete, however, is the relationship (historical, political and eco-nomic as well as geomorphic) between the Americas and Eurasi-africa—and particularly today, while human civilization is still pre-dominantly "north-hemispheric", between North-America (includ-ing what is unfortunately called Central America) and Eurasia. *Global harmony and international peace depend almost entirely upon the type of relationship and interchange established between these two complementary masses of land and of humanity;* and most of the problems we face today are due to the fact that, in 1919-20, the

American Senate and the American people at large refused to assume the responsibility of such a permanent relationship, while supporting and helping a long-winded attempt to crush Soviet Russia and thwart her evident historical and geographical destiny in any integral and globally organized humanity.

We are not referring here to the communist ideology or the political methods of the Soviets. We are speaking of concrete and realistic facts of geography and history, and of nothing else. Basically, it is these facts which determine, if not political systems and cultural ideals in themselves, at least their failure or success in establishing themselves on a particular soil. Likewise, the supremacy of England in world-politics was founded upon the fact that she, as an insular outpost of Europe to the west, was in position to use preeminently and to capitalize upon the gold and cotton of America, and to merchandize and transport across the seas much of America's wealth, especially after Spain's downfall. Now, however, that the Americas are becoming definitely established as one of the poles of a global economy, and that Soviet Russia has aroused to productive activity the central regions of Eurasia, the role of England is becoming unnecessary in terms of geotechnics—even if it can be still considered very important in the realm of spiritual values and world-civilization; provided the English people can focus their creative energy there.

The role of French culture can be similarly understood in terms of the fact that France links the Northern seas, the Atlantic and the Mediterranean, and is the westernmost outlet of Eurasia—more so than Spain, whose geotechnical significance resides in her position as the western point of contact between Africa and Europe, this fact having predestined her to be the seat of the great Mozarabic culture and thus a most important link between the Near East and France at a crucial time of European history (around 900 A.D.). France is, by her position, a natural outpost for the Russian hinterland of Europe, being the point of convergence of Northern, Central and Mediterranean Europe—and as well of North Africa; and in as much as a passively polarized Africa responds to an active and positive Europe, France's control over West North Africa—from Tunisia to the Congo, with Dakar as a center—was an inevitable geotechnical result. For the same reason, Russia is bound, sooner or later, to expand her influence over Egypt and the Arab world, England's hegemony there being a transitional factor which must lose its basic importance as a global polarization becomes fully established between the U.S.S.R. and the U.S.A. The connection between India and the whole of South Africa is also a matter of geotechnical inevitability, and Gandhi's life is a symbol of this fact.

Polarities in World-Politics

Triangular North America and crescent-shape Eurasia are today as man and woman in the great ritual of full global production; and much of what we have written concerning the relationship between man and woman as consciously productive polarities could apply basically to what the relation between U.S.A. and U.S.S.R. *should be.* But it never can be a creative relationship in terms of physical and spiritual abundance until the American people come to discover and fully accept their world-destiny *as releasers of a new civilizing spirit*—a new logos. Which means, first of all, until the American people overcome their collective adolescent mother-complex, and American men come into their own as positive civilizing agents outside of the field of merely *physical* business productivity and management.

As long as the post-war search for nylon stockings, the glamour type of Movies and the sentimentality of Jazz-song can be construed the world over as typical of the American psyche—as long as most of American culture, literature, music and art still looks to Europe for old classical patterns and bows to commercial motives—America proves herself as unready psychologically as politically to assume her evident part of destiny in the global harmony of an integrated humanity. And as long as this is so, the Eurasian matrix is left un-impregnated by the new descent of creative spirit; is left to develop her new structures of society on the sole basis of the old vibration of earth-culture, instead of as the result of a creative inter-play between a new spiritual descent of power and this ancient earth-culture. Culture needs to be periodically fecundated by civi-lization; Fire must stimulate creative mutations in Seed—and Ameri-ca must today release this new Fire to make Eurasiafrica great with a global progeny.

America has just released this new Fire *in its physical aspect and in terms of destruction; but in no other way as yet.* As a cathartic purifying fire over a Sodom-like Hiroshima the atom's power made sense. As a threat against Eurasia, it is a symbol of male bullying. American democracy can not be imposed upon Eurasia under the menace of atomic bombs or the coercion of loans. The Bikini show will remain a symbol of psychological bungling and political double-talk, as well as of uncontrolled and unsavory publicity, in which the American way of life was presented in a most doubtful light. America has to offer a great deal of "fire" to the old world; this, she publicizes hugely. But the "light" that noble and creative Americans have emanated is clouded and misunderstood, as well as repudiated by overt acts that give our great phrases the lie. A fa-mous religious leader recently spoke of the "American schizophre-nia"; a historian of earlier days wrote an essay entitled "America: *Facts vs. Phrases"*. This means a deep lack of inner integration and a latent or overt psychological conflict in our national life.

The "light" is there, but it is the immature and uncertain light of adolescence; and there is grave danger always in such a case that the new "fire" discovered by the youth may be led into destructive explosions, rather than toward the state of illumination. Both the United States and Soviet Russia are adolescent giants who are still growing into their respective collective and integral personalities—each according to a definite rhythm of social progress. These two rhythms essentially complement each other; indeed, between these two countries one can easily detect the very same type of misunderstandings, distrust and confused relationship based on escapism, fear and pride which exist between boy and girl trying to make themselves ready to enter into a new world of mature responsibility—especially with relatives and jealous friends or neighbors introducing elements of complexity and confusion.

We stress here the United States and Soviet Russia because they represent the concrete foci of organizing and productive power in the world of tomorrow; as is becoming increasingly evident. Even the British Empire is gradually taking on the character of a screen used by the real managers of U. S. diplomacy to cover up ultimate goals —and so also is China made to serve American interests. And Russia is answering such a policy in her own traditional manner, a typically "feminine" manner—witness the methods her representatives use both in Eastern European countries and in diplomatic meetings. And by "feminine" we do not mean soft or subtle! Woman's nature has her own typical methods of intimidation and her own brand of ruthlessness, psychic and otherwise—a brand exemplified throughout the ages by the behavior of all big religious organizations under stress, and particularly in this case by the techniques of the medieval Church, with its militant Orders and its Inquisition, its dogmatism and appeal to collective fear.

Because we find today the two great centers of a global humanity demonstrating many of the negative characteristics of the polarities of human nature which they represent, because their collective (and above all, governmental) attitudes to the use of power emphasize on the surface un-constructive elements, this does *not* mean that an open conflict between the two dominant protagonists of our twentieth century world is to be expected. And much of the responsibility for removing the possibility of such a conflict, whose results would be almost beyond conception, rest upon the older nations of the world. These nations may not be any longer determinants in the new global world of productive power, but they can and should exert a basic influence in the realm of meaning and spiritual values.

Power of itself has neither meaning nor truly human value. It results from a more or less organized interplay of unconscious forces and natural activities which follows *cosmic* patterns but not *spiritual* goals. "Purpose" is potentially implied in "form," but unless this spirit-directed purpose is expressed by conscious individuals and cultural groups in clear and convincing statements, it remains inoperative, and power mushrooms forth in spiritual blindness, merely following the line of least resistance outlined by the structural patterns of human instincts and old societies.

America and Soviet Russia have an enormous potential of energy, as healthy adolescents have. The power which already floods their collective organisms manifests in polar ways—in an individualistic, heterogeneous and mostly aimless manner in the United States; in a collectivistic, centrally determined and psychologically tense and self-conscious way in Soviet Russia. In both cases, *power determines its own release,* even though resonant phrases and high ideals adorn the actual behavior of the real managers of power. This is an inevitable characteristic of adolescence: the youth is led by his or her life-instincts and power-urges, and is unable as yet to control them. In fact the adolescent has no objective perspective upon these natural forces, and thus is normally bewildered by them, whether he follows them blindly or he recoils in fear and moral indignation from them.

The American people at large are bewildered by the atomic energy with which they have been confronted, just as a young man with a particularly violent sex-passion. They do not even understand clearly—they did not grasp it at all in 1919—what the power and responsibility of their own wealth imply; and much of their isolationism has been based on a real fear of foreign entanglements and on a vivid sense of inferiority in all international dealings.

Soviet Russia is in a similar or corresponding psychological state; one might say symbolically like a young girl ruled by a rigid traditional fear of the bad boy, capitalism, and by an unpredictable "woman pride"—combined with a genuine yearning for international comradeship and the deep urge to gather to her womb all seed and all past. Whether that urge is interpreted as absorption for self-aggrandizement, or redemption from social evil . . . depends entirely upon one's social philosophy! Objectively speaking, both interpretations seem correct in view of the mental-psychological confusion of adolescence; just as it is true to speak of American idealism and American imperialism in the same breath.

Such conflicting motives are obviously to be met with in all countries. But, while the conflict and confusion is natural and relatively inevitable in vast and young national organisms, this should not be so in older collectivities, especially like France and England, with waning instinctual powers, very mature cultures, and highly developed individuals with innate mental skill and breadth of vision. The problem for such countries is how to rise above their "glorious traditions" and deliberately re-focus the national consciousness and sense of responsibility *from the realm of collective power (imperialism) to that of individualized spiritual purpose and meaning.* It is the problem attending the "change of life" in the individual man and woman: how to make old age significant in terms of spirit, instead of instincts. And leaders like Churchill and de Gaulle symbolize the stubborn refusal of some sections of their nations to accept the change—a clinging to national, religious and cultural traditions which today have no longer real meaning *unless* they are re-polarized and transmuted by a spiritual purpose.

What is this purpose? It is the release of "seed-men" who should spiritually fecundate the as yet inchoate societies of America and Central Eurasia, and give a spiritual meaning and direction to the immense productive power with which these societies are charged. This fecundation, however, if it is to be constructive and really spiritual in a progressive evolutionary sense, must not be based on a philosophy and life-attitude stemming from thirteenth century thought (Neo-Thomism and the like). All the "Neo" philosophies, religious or cultural, are regressive—even, if they may contain elements of great value. These elements, however, can only become vital and significant parts of a truly fecund and progressive world-viewpoint *after* they have become basically re-oriented and transfigured by a new descent of the spirit. Without this spiritual impregnation, there can be no true civilizing "seed"—but, instead, a kind of cancerous or inorganic growth. And we know now that the chemical components of both procreative substances and dangerous growths are very similar. The one difference is that mysterious essence of life or spirit which either is or is not present in the substance.

One Ocean for the One World

All this means that there can be no progressive and spirit-conditioned human future, for individuals and collectivities alike, unless a process of metamorphosis (repolarization and transfiguration) is experienced. This is the process which ancient civilizations in Asia, Egypt or Greece described under the symbolism of Initiations into the greater Mysteries. It is the process allegorized in the great events of the New Testament drama, from John the Baptist's call to inner metamorphosis *(metanoia)* to the Baptism, Transfiguration, Crucifixion-Resurrection and Ascension of the embodied Christ. It is the process to which modern psychologists such as Carl Jung and Fritz Kunkel refer under the name of the "process of individuation."

This process must be experienced by humanity at large before the future Age of plenitude can become a global and all-inclusive reality. It is a long process, we can safely assume; how long, we dare not say. But we are undoubtedly correct in saying that the historical period we are living in, since the Revolutionary era of the late eighteenth century, since the Industrial Revolution of one hundred years ago, and still more since the real beginning of World War II with Japan's invasion of Manchuria (September 1931), has all the characteristics of such a collective human metamorphosis.

We might even significantly relate the American and French Revolutions to a John the Baptist's call to self-reorientation and "repentance." The Industrial Revolution of the 1840-50 decade (with the synchronous birth of religious movements, from Babism and Bahaism in Persia to American Spiritualism and Christian Science, and including the social religions of the German Marx and of the French Humanitarians, St. Simon, Fourier, Comte) would represent the symbolical Baptism of the new humanity, with (as its negative result) the proud ego-expansiveness of nationalistic imperialism and "rugged individualism." The Transfiguration might be connected with the end of last century and some of its deeper thought-currents, and especially with the discovery of radio-activity and Einstein's new world-vision. And we might be plunged into the phase of the Crucifixion, with the release of atomic energy (actually a release of spirit from the binding structures of matter) as a *promise* of Resurrection.

We should only consider it a "promise," as far as collective humanity is concerned. The United Nations *may* become in time the true "Risen Body" of a federated global humanity, delivered from the bonds of a nationalism made destructive by the concept of absolute "national sovereignty" (the ego-principle in collective human organisms). But even the few Apostles who knew Christ so well took some time to admit He had risen, and far longer to understand the meaning of what they had witnessed. And it will be some time undoubtedly before men understand all that has happened since 1931, and the world-significance of personages like Roosevelt and Hitler, of events like the collapse and resurgence of France, the rise of the U.S.S.R. as a matrix for a future Eurasiatic culture, etc.

What we are facing today is a new global birth of human society, based on new (because untried) principles of human relation-

ship. And the great symbol of this gradual emergence of a new
world is the *one ocean, matrix for the one world.* All birthing is
out of some "sea." And as long as men could conceive only of
separate seas with distinguishing names, or at best of "the seven
seas," it was impossible for the "one world" to be born. But now,
thanks to our global and total war, men have come to consider all
seas as one ocean, and to visualize the earth as a globe. In terms
of this new geographical sense Soviet Russia and North America
have become close neighbors *whose bodies encircle the North Pole
and its star*—a great and profound symbol, indeed!

One ocean, and out of it two vast continental masses fanning
out from the North Pole. Humanity speeds now through this one
ocean and its atmospheric counterpart; breathes the one air which
unites all individuals and nations, even the most proud isolationists;
is nervously and visually stimulated by sounds and pictures which
fill the radio strata with the chaos and the yearnings of confused
and insecure, but aspiring and aroused collectivities. As men travel
swiftly from continent to continent, even a large continent can be
seen as one huge island; and as men's minds listen to radio music
and voices from many races and nations, and see on the screen
people of various colors and features perform daily tasks conditioned by the common humanity of all, they gradually realize that
all nations, large or small, are like islands of consciousness and
culture emerged from the one ocean of man's generic and collective
unconscious.

Consciousness and culture polarize the topology of continents;
civilization and geomorphics deal with one basic reality from two
angles. The developing body of human traditions and achievements,
through the long eras of human evolution, is forever rooted in the
shifting masses of sun-illumined and rain-moistened land. One
should no more seek to dissolve islands into the ocean than to merge
the varied cultures into a collective sea of uniform and impersonal
responses to standardized global living. The goal of a global human-

ity is organicity, not monotony. Because there is one single ocean as the matrix for the one world of Man, this does not mean that men will have to make of this watery expanse their abode! Man can be said symbolically to emerge, in his global Avatar, *from* this one ocean; nevertheless the new global world is not to be a world of sameness, but instead a world in which every island and continent is related to each other in depth, yet in individualized distinctiveness — as the many varieties of trees in a forest are related through the soil which feeds and sustains their roots, yet each rises to the sun in its own characteristic way and gives out its own seed.

The relationship between individual personalities and Man, as we have defined it in the beginning of this book, parallels that between nations and global humanity. We did not present as our basic new goal the ideal of impersonality, but instead that of the transpersonal life. Likewise we do not envision for tomorrow the absorption of nations into a vast super-state controlling all humanity under one enforced set of laws, but we present as the next evolutionary goal the ideal of "transnationalism"—the application to the realm of *national* personalities of the ideals of the transpersonal life which we have outlined in relation to *individual* personalities.

The Transnational Way

When one faces a condition of generalized crisis, the temptation is always to evade the problem at home by rushing to establish a new and bigger set of rules to which everybody else also should conform; and if anyone seems reluctant to accept the rules, he is loudly blamed for whatever evil may develop. This is colloquially called "passing the buck"—or, in modern psychology, "projecting one's Shadow" upon a conveniently placed relative, friend or foe.

In other words, if you cannot solve your personal problem and repair the old mistakes which contributed to chaos in your surroundings, you join a "great Cause" (religious or social) and submit to an external discipline in which your own problems are (temporarily) absorbed; while keeping ready to pounce eagerly upon anyone who is not so sure of the long range value of the Cause and, either fails to join in, or breaks some rule. "Impersonality," strictly speaking, is not the state which follows the successful demonstration of a warm creative personality; it is the refuge for men who could not meet all the tests of personality and found it easier to become absorbed into some larger whole, in the management of which they have only a small share, or none at all.

It is for such reasons usually that frightened or bewildered intellectuals join some ancient and apparently most stable Church, or enlist in a crusade against some monstrous social evil in comparison to which their own personal failings and bad temper become truly insignificant. A similar psychological background accounts in many cases for the eagerness of some of the best minds of our day to establish a "world-government" which would create a set body of world-laws controlling the bad temper and duplicity of all nations, thus establishing a crucially needed sense of security.

That there should arise a true World-Federation of Nations within a relatively short time is the obvious consequence of all that has been said in this book. The next step ahead for humanity is some kind of world-federalism and world-organization of all human resources toward the goal of full productivity for all and by all. This, we have stated again and again. However, we have also pointed out in our first chapter that by relying solely or most heavily upon *institutions,* and by shirking the far more basic need for the personal and mental-spiritual metamorphosis of *individuals and nations,* our present-day humanity may very well take the road to the abyss—the type of road which the old Roman Empire took.

It has become highly fashionable among intellectuals to point out with awed reverence to the two centuries of the *Pax Romana* from Augustus on, and to the fact that during these centuries one could travel unmolested from Spain to Syria. This argument sounds suspiciously like the statements of not so long ago that Italian

Fascism was great because Mussolini made the trains run on time, drained the swamps near Rome and removed beggars from the streets! And where now is Mussolini and this wonderful new order which he imposed upon his people? And what happened before to the Roman Empire of the Caesars, most of whom were dissolute wretches reigning by the grace of an Army and of ruthless administrators who were the real rulers?

This glorification of the *Pax Romana* is a kind of specious propaganda for a new type of world-Fascism. Not only did the first century A.D. witness the persecutions of the Christians and the rise of a Roman society, artificial and without any human depth—and obviously quite similar to "high society" of our Western civilization before and after our World-Wars—; but even this very first century of the "greatness that was Rome" saw revolts in Gaul, in Germany, in Palestine, and already typical Army revolutions. Trajan and other emperors did build magnificent buildings, bridges and roads throughout the empire; and there were great gladiators games in Rome. But after the noble and wise Marcus Aurelius who died in 180, the empire was practically in the control of Army factions fighting periodically for supremacy, while the high society disintegrated and finally turned Christian out of sheer spiritual emptiness. By 375 A.D. the great Roman show was all over—to be revived less than a thousand years later with the trappings of "holiness." Did the ghost of the Holy Roman Empire, which inspired Napoleon and Hitler, vanish with the bombing of Berlin and with the Potsdam Conference—or is it being enlarged and redecorated for use in a bigger and better empire of the world?

To build greater institutions without greater human beings to ensoul them can be a dangerous procedure. There may be no other alternatives when the need for such institutions is inescapable; but when the world is bringing forth potential imperators and Coliseums, let us not forget that their only spiritual value resides in that they may help unwillingly the eventual spread of a new Christ-spirit;

and let us not take for granted that a world-government in the hands
of unregenerate men would be "democratic"—even if under American control! Social problems are not solved by extending the field
of social organization. Men are not transfigured by organizations.
It is organizations which have to be transfigured by men.

What we have called the "transpersonal way" is the way of per-
sonality-transfiguration. Following it, an individual transforms his
attitude to life, to himself and to humanity. Because he is able to
realize himself as an agent through whom Man creates and evolution pursues its progress toward ultimate and spirit-conditioned
goals, the transpersonal human being can meet with other human
beings in terms of fully conscious, lucid and productive companionship. As a "companion" his whole being is sustained by the "living Bread" of truth and understanding, by his rootedness in man's
common humanity and his utter consecration to the seed-consummation of Man in a truly living and creative civilization. As a companion he is also a "server," able to manage, as a sacred trust, the
power released by humanity as a whole and by his own particular
social community. And together with the "co-servers" who complement him, he is able to constitute a true Civil Service adminis-
trating for Man the wealth of the earth and of all that live thereon
toward the establishment of the Age of plenitude and of creative
fulfillment in all realms.

If this be the picture of the new individual person toward which
human evolution is leading, then a corresponding image should be
outlined revealing the meaning and function of the *new nation* in
the atomic Age—if there are still to be nations in the centuries
ahead. But should nations continue to exist? And what is actually
and fundamentally a nation? The answers to these questions are not
to be taken for granted. Indeed, modern man's mind is quite confused as to the implications and the value of the concept of "nation," as the history of the last decades proves.

First of all, a nation is not a tribe, or a group of related tribes; and it is not an empire. It is not a tribal unit and it is not even a racial unit. One of the greatest and most characteristic fallacies at the root of Nazism was the idea that a nation was a social organism including one single racial strain and vitalized by one "pure" blood. Such an idea is historically ridiculous and spiritually meaningless. Nations, in the accurate sense of the term, constitute a very recent type of social development, and one can say that France was the first nation in history (it became a nation after Joan of Arc, thus around 500 years ago; England followed, then Spain).

A nation can be defined, on historical grounds, as the result of the integration of two, three, or even more racial groups and traditions within well defined geographical boundaries and on the basis of a common language and culture—or at least an officially predominant language and culture. Philosophically speaking, we shall define a nation as: a *formative field* within which a particular basic type of human beings is developed and maintained, with an infinite number of individual and group variations.

We have implied that a nation was a collective personality; but actually we consider humanity as a whole as the only real and stable collective personality correlated with the one globe of the earth, more or less as the individual psyche and mind are correlated with a physical human body. A nation (with its language, culture and institutions) is a formative field for the development of a type of individuals whose basic destiny is to fulfill *a particular function* in the total economy of humanity as a whole. It is not a tribe because it is not a merely bio-psychic entity completely bound to the earth, as flora and fauna to soil and climate. It is a formative field —a training school, we might almost say—for the establishment of a *style* of mental and psychic human production, at all levels. This field is definitely influenced by geography, land resources and climates, yet it is not merely the progeny of it. It is there in order to serve a functional purpose in terms of the ultimate all-human and global synthesis, Man.

For this reason, a nation is the result of the integration of, at the very least, two dominant racial strains, and probably, in principle, three. It is a "hybrid" conditioned by the need of humanity as a whole for a special kind or style of human productivity; much as a new species of plants is created by hybridization in order to meet the need for a product with definite characteristics, such as early maturity, large flowers, resistance to bad weather, heavy seed-output, etc.

What is it that directs the process of hybridization? No answer can be given here that would satisfy all schools of thought. We may say it is God's purpose and postulate intelligent Agents serving that purpose. At any rate, it is presumably the same type of agencies or directing will which control the development of oaks from acorns, and organize the most intricate interdependence of glands, nerve and organs in human behavior. Certain tribal groups are seemingly impelled to move toward definite geographical areas, there to settle and intermingle. What made the Arabs settle in Spain from the south some centuries after the Visigoths came from the north, both blending with indigenous races and a number of colonists from various Mediterranean countries? Spain was the result of the hybridization of these racial collectivities; as the French nation and culture resulted from the blending of Celts, Germans, Vikings and Mediterranean races, and Great Britain from the union of Celt, Anglo-Saxon and Scandinavians. But who can tell whether it was not the *archetypal function,* "Spain," that *drew* to the square peninsula jutting westward out of Eurasia the Arabs, the Visigoths, and other colonizing groups—just as it is the function of human vision which draws the fibres of optic nerves and all the substances in the eye to that locality in the human body best suited to be the seat of such a function!

Considered in such a light, nations are seen to have significance and value essentially in terms of the contribution which the individuals and groups they bring forth make to the total economy— material and spiritual—of humanity as an organic whole, as a global personality. These individuals are usually at first unconscious of the fact that their productions serve a definite functional purpose in a global civilization which they cannot even visualize; and as a result, nations keep fighting each other in often senseless ambition for more wealth or more "living space." However, a day comes when individuals who in every nation have vision and understanding at last realize that humanity is an organic whole, that each nation has a functional destiny in this whole and that it should have as its essential dynamic purpose to contribute its collective style of life and characteristic temperament to the gradual formation of Man, the seedhood of humanity.

When this occurs and the national life is reoriented accordingly, then the ideal of "transnationalism" becomes an operative fact. Every nation sees itself and acts as a creative agent *through* whom Man moves toward his multifarious seed-fulfillment. Then, the effective companionship of nations can begin, and humanity is on the way to become a global personality. Then, world-management can operate in terms of international cooperation and productive harmony, because every nation is ready to *serve* the purpose of the whole of humanity.

World-management, world-service—but not what is unfortunately named world-government! Government implies politics and laws which usually play into the hands of those who formulate them full of clever loopholes. *The one imperative need of our day is the substitution of management to politics and, as a prerequisite, of consecrated service to self-righteous sovereignty.*

We are dealing here—we should emphasize it strongly—with problems of production. A nation is a formative field or a training ground for productive personalities. Production is a matter of management, not of politics. The curse of politics should at last be lifted up from the souls of men—and it is as well the curse of ego-centricity and absolute sovereignty. The only true sovereignty is sovereignty over one's own nature. It is not a matter of superiority over (of power over) other individuals or nations. And yet this concept of "superiority over" is found in the very root of the word, sovereignty, and actually it expresses the subconscious drive underneath the subsequent and secondary meaning of self-determination and independence of will. No will has ever been independent in a vacuum. Sovereignty is either a value of protest (the weak seeking to protect himself from the powerful), or a value of over-lordship (the powerful making it very sure no one questions his right to prove his superiority throughout "zones of influence"). Will men ever stop deceiving themselves with verbalisms, and face squarely the one basic issue confronting them: either to serve a superpersonal purpose, or to pull to oneself for self-aggrandize-ment and to absorb whatever can be set loose from its roots?

The ultimate choice is between creative companionship or tyran-nical absorption to self. It is a white and black alternative, and the two poles are "harmony" and "war." Law is a poor substi-tute for harmony, because law implies potential warfare and con-flicts between individuals who reluctantly give up some of their ego-characteristics or sovereign rights. Law is necessary at a certain stage of human evolution, but it is a makeshift—indeed, basically, a mere fallacy. Any formulated law is bound by the very act of formulation—by the "letter of the law."

Harmony, on the other hand, is a fact of the spiritual life, the transpersonal life. It is a structural fact founded in root-unity and seed-purpose—a purpose to which all the chorded individuals or nations have dedicated their all. Harmony belongs to the realm of the psychology of the living human person; law, to that of insti-tutions and of classes of entities such as science studies. The only approach to world-redemption from war, destructive competition, greed and jealousy is essentially a psychological approach—simply because all these personal and social curses are all by-products of human fear. Only psychology, harmony, love, understanding can eradicate or transmute fear.

We do not mean these words as sentimental fetishes or verbalistic ideals. We think of them in terms of practical and concrete procedures, in terms of definite educational activities, in terms of radical social reforms in all fields—education, economics, religion, literature, etc. We think of them in terms of the evident and inescapable fact that there can be no world-peace and global civilization unless psychological harmony—not governmental law— is established between the two basic polarities of the new humanity: individualistic North America and collectivistic Soviet Russia. And there can be no harmony established between these two operative poles and productive halves of our "one world," until we, Americans, who should be, by geographical and spiritual destiny, the positive pole of the "marriage" radiate creative harmony. But we cannot radiate harmony until we ourselves overcome our sentimental weaknesses, our collective mother complex, our repeated efforts to whitewash ourselves and our past, our "passing the buck" and hypocritical self-shielding under big phrases; until we can control and disarm these forces in American society which, for lack of any psychological understanding and maturity, are bent upon world-domination, hatred, distrust . . . and the use of the atomic bomb, if and when.

The spectacle of the United States "way of life" since the fateful death of Franklin D. Roosevelt and our occupation of enemy territory is not an inspiring one. And it makes no difference that the way other nations behaved has been no more edifying. The Buddha said: Hatred does not cease by hatred, but by love. And today we should state, by deeds and not in double-talk, that fear in others can never be eradicated by brandishing our superior wealth and power, atomic or otherwise, but by spreading goodwill and not tolerating ill-will in high places or the subtle propaganda of a money-controlled press and radio. We have played power-politics as hard as anyone else, both officially and through unofficial groups which, whether we like it or not, represent America in the international world as much as, and often more than, our diplomatic agents. And the game can go on just as well within a world-government as without it, when this super-government is constituted as the result of fear, and little else.

The craving for security under law can never guarantee peace within an institution built upon such a craving. The pressure of fear may cement blocs of nations; it cannot generate the connective tissues which surround the organs of a living organism. We must not deceive ourselves. If the real ruling-groups in the United States join a world-government it will be with the aim of perpetuating more securely our business ascendancy. If England does so, it will be to seek the maintenance of a minimum of empire which, without strong props, would naturally collapse. If small nations accept an over-all world-government, it will be because they have nothing really to lose and much to gain. And if Soviet Russia follows suit, it will be because she hopes to gain by political infiltration a position of stronger power than that which she now has, as the only communistic country among nations dominated by generally hostile ruling classes.

This entire book and all our previous writings anywhere should show that we are most definitely *for* world-organization and rapid world-federation; but we feel it necessary to emphasize today that no institution, especially if based on fear, can insure global harmony. No marriage, however lawful and formal, is a guarantee against divorce or conjugal warfare. No world-government can insure against a Civil War of Man. We *are* indeed today in the midst of such a Civil War, at least since 1932. Can we honestly ignore this fact? We are actually in the midst of a war of religions. And to such a type of war today, there can be only two solutions: harmony or exhaustion on both sides. Are we not historically minded enough to realize that when a civil war ends (as the American Civil War did) in the destruction of one side by the other, the victor becomes spiritually or psychologically crippled for a long time? How different perhaps would be the world today if there had not been a Southern bloc of Senators (heir to Civil War attitudes) to oppose Franklin D. Roosevelt and to focus the impact of social reaction and racial prejudice! How different would be America, had the cultures of the South and the North become integrated in creative interplay and productive, resonant harmony!

The North and the South were meant as functional polarities in one great nation. Because one pole was blighted the spiritual disease of commercialism and materialism spread over the United States. Our nation has become powerful; it has not recovered as yet from the Civil War's aftermath. There was civil war between the successors of the murdered Caesar, and Augustus won; but while the Roman Empire was powerful, it never knew the inner harmony that is spiritually creative. Today the world contains several polarized nations or national groups which must be harmonized and integrated, if there is to be global peace and full all-human productivity. And among these polar couplings none is more basic than the one embracing the U.S.A. and the U.S.S.R.—also the coupling of North and South America.

The victory of one polarity over the other can never be productive. No victory that does not include the defeated is ever real. Harmony alone is reality. It alone leads to the full harvest, to the completeness of Man. The rule of law is empty without the substance of harmony. Integration by political law is no living and organic integration. It is coercion; not "co-action." And if we are to have a global society in terms of creative fullness of being, we have to repolarize and renew utterly our concept of law.

The Hindu philosopher speaks of *dharma;* and by *dharma* he means the inherent functional character of an organism, the "truth" of it; thus, the fulfillment of God's purpose that brought it into being. To live the life of *dharma* is to fulfill the innate potentiality of one's own nature—to be purely what one is, and nothing else. It is to perform inherently necessary acts, to actualize in fully mature personality the individual Identity that is one's function or place in the universal Whole, and in Man.

This, we already mentioned while discussing the "transpersonal way" and the reality of freedom. And practically all of that discussion can be repeated at the level of nations. Far more even than a personality, a nation has no meaning or human value except with reference to the whole of humanity. A nation is solely a functional unit within the organic whole of humanity, for humanity—we repeat—is the only permanent collective personality. Every other kind of legally recognized "collective person," from a business corporation to a nation, has only a functional significance. And it is a great legalistic fallacy, inherited from the Roman Law, to consider such a collective social personality as a "sovereign" entity having absolute value in itself. *Outside of humanity as a whole, there are no collective persons, in the real sense of the term "person"; there are only collective functions or units of management.*

A nation should be considered, both, as a "unit of management" within a global economy, and as a "training school" for a certain basic type of individual personalities, of styles of life and of cultural activity. And we do not say this with the intention of belittling the concept of nation. There must be nations; but not as absolute persons. There must be nations because *functional differentiation* is necessary, in order to insure the fullest possible human production. Functional differentiation implies polarization of related functional units. Nations are thus functional polarities. And global humanity can only be based upon the harmonic interplay of these polar rhythms of human behavior and creativeness.

What is needed in order to establish such a harmonic interplay may be called "law"; but it should be more significantly named "structural planning." Law implies one-sided coercion; structural planning implies, at first, constructing imagination, then (when in operation) reciprocity in action. These two factors, constructing imagination and reciprocal activity, are the foundations of the new world and the new society we envision; as they are likewise the foundations of any productive and spiritually transfiguring relationship between a man and a woman in polarized companionship. Mutuality is the essence of creative production, and the soul of mutuality is love in truth; love, the substance of the Holy Spirit that is the spirit of truth (considered as *dharma*) and understanding (i.e. the realization of a common foundation which "stands under" all differentiated individual traits).

Real management can never exist without mutuality; that is, without functional give-and-take. True managers are men who believe in, and practice mutuality. And mutuality is the very keynote of the teachings of Christ: a mutuality which is no longer a matter of unconscious instinct and complex organic response, but which is established at the level of conscious personality in the "love of the companions." It is such a mutuality which is needed in the international world as it is needed in modern marriages. World-government is good, if pervaded with it. World-government can only mean world-empire or a constant state of global Civil War, if it is not substantiated by this mutuality and this love in truth and understanding which alone can insure creative harmony and world-management for full human productivity, by all and for all.

The atomic bomb—our American child—compels us to seek at once world-government. But we should not consider this world-government as a panacea for peace—which it can not be *of itself*. It is a container. And a container has vital significance only in terms of its contents. Men who try to build the container should be encouraged and assisted. But their task would be futile, at best, unless the just as important work of providing living and spiritual contents goes on at the same time—and, preferably, precedes the erection of the world-structure.

WORLD MANAGEMENT:
The Human Need, Purpose and Planning

"And how shall we go about doing this?"—the reader may ask. The only possible answer, here, is that it is all a matter of conscious and effective management, on the basis of a philosophy of life inclusive in scope, harmonic in method, and spiritual in purpose. No preestablished rule can be formulated to apply in any one particular case, and no law can be established except the law of maximum inclusiveness and harmony—and this is a "principle", rather than a "law".

According to our philosophical and metaphysical understanding, spirit operates in answer to a need. Creation is not the "play" (in Sanskrit, *Lila*) of a God demonstrating Himself to Himself; it is— if considered in terms of time-sequence and cyclic activity (as man is always bound actually to consider it)—the cyclic integration of three cosmic factors: spirit (or activity), form, and substance (or matter). Each of these three cosmic factors has its own distinct rhythm and essential character. But while none of them can or should become absorbed into the other and lose its character, all three can and should operate in harmony within That which, at the same time, encompasses them and forever seeks to integrate them while keeping each distinct and "pure" according to its own character or *dharma*. We may call "That", Space or God, or with Hindu mystics TAT. The name is relatively unimportant, provided the basic concept is clear.

This concept is not only metaphysical and abstract; it is also most practical, in as much as it is the very core of all *management*. A factory in operation, for instance, is essentially a field of "activity" within which "substance" is being given a characteristic "form".

The factory operates, moreover, in order to fill definite *needs* (need of the community for certain products, need of the workers and managers for living wages, etc). It operates according to a definite *plan,* procedure and schedule, determined by a *purpose*—which is, the fulfillment of the needs of all the human beings concerned.

According to the purely monistic idea of creation, spirit expresses itself through substance as well as through form, both of which it creates out of itself. Why it should create them is however a forever unexplained and obviously unexplainable mystery. There can be no human reason for it, and the idea of it is in itself unconceivable. We believe, indeed, that it is the result of a psychological compensation rooted in the ego-glorification and sheer absolutism of the "I"; also, the result of social conditions prevailing in highly ritualized and "planned" societies, for instance, the Brahminical or Mosaic societies. And this absolute monism seems to involve a basic confusion of terms or levels.

Instead, it is our understanding that the *essence* of substance and form is indestructible, just as spirit is indestructible. What changes is the type of relationship between them. The *harmony* is constantly modified; and as it is modified, each of the three basic components of this harmony takes on greatly different characteristics. We say, for instance, that the atom explodes and that matter is transformed into energy according to the famous Einsteinian formula, $E=MC^2$. Matter is not destroyed, however. It is "transformed"; i..e. its relationship to the element of "form" is altered. But whether as energy within the universal ocean of "power" in spheroidal space, or as a matter within the form defined by atomic structure, it is still what we call "substance".

Likewise, in any operation of human management, the substances used in the operation are only transformed—whether they be mined ore, the wood of cut trees, the scrap iron of junk piles, or electric current and coal. The substance used may also be mental; as when a composer of music transforms the notes of traditional scales (his raw materials) into a symphony, or when the violinist sets into toneful vibration the molecules of his violin-strings, or when a philosopher or mathematician gives new ideological form to the word-pictures and conceptual relationships which he inherited from his culture.

All such operations imply management. A "substance" found by the manager in a certain state of "form" (i.e. of relationship with other substances within physical or mental boundaries) is transformed (i.e. given a new form) in order to meet a definite need. The transforming agent is a man, who either acts from his own isolated ego-center or, as an agent for Man, in terms of his inclusive Self united in companionship to all likewise inclusive human Selves.

Life, and the entire universal process, constitute cyclic series of transformations. And, in our view, God is, both, the manager and the container of these transformations. He is both spirit—the source of the transforming activity—and space—the vessel within which the transformation occurs. Man is likewise spirit and space; and by space, here, we mean the electro-magnetic *field* (the so-called "aura") within which all the processes of transformation which forever modify his physical and psycho-mental organism (his total personality) occur. Humanity—as we consider it—also is spirit and space; its spirit is "Man," its space is the earth-globe with all its atmospheric layers—and it may even be said to include the entire orbital space of the earth's revolution around its source of light and life, the sun.

Management, thus, from its most metaphysical to its most practical spheres of operation, can be defined as *transforming activity according to plan, within a definite space, in order to fill a well-defined need.* Thus described management is, in practice, determined, not only by the need it must fill, but also by the space available and by the materials at hand which are to be transformed. It is determined further by the type of forms—i.e. plans for finished products, blue-prints, or "archetypes"—which can be obtained.

This being understood, what does humanity require in order to manage effectively and successfully the transformation from the old order of scarcity to the muture order of plenitude? Humanity requires a clear understanding of man's needs, of the global space in which it can operate, of the materials and the workers available for the needed transformation, of the end-results (thus, the purpose) of the transforming process. When such a clear understanding is obtained, then a workable plan and schedule of operation can be devised; if not all at once, at least by progressive stages, as the occasion requires.

It should be obvious that there is today no such "clear understanding" in men who govern officially the nations of our contemporary world. There is likewise no such clear understanding in evidence among the recognized and traditional cultural, educational or religious leaders in any nation. Is it astonishing therefore that humanity is today in a state of chaos and menaced by nearly total destruction? The cause of it is: lack of effective management, resulting from the lack of human vision and of an understanding of all factors required for world-management.

Three factors must be recognized and related in any situation which calls for real management: need, purpose and planning. And as we deal with human values and with the destiny of the whole mankind, these three basic factors call into play the activities of three corresponding types of mentalities: the psychologist, the creative philosopher or religious prophet, the scientist and manager.

The Need. Psychology is a way of understanding human needs. Some of these needs appear to be strictly biological; yet it should be quite evident that when biological needs are not satisfied the result, in terms of human behavior, is psychological. Even the most obviously biological and material of all needs, the need for food to keep alive, is presented to us in these post-war years of famine, as having to be met for the reason that famine breeds despair, revolution and communism! That people should die of hunger does not seem to be as important as the psychological—and political— results of starvation. And it has been said that one of the values of organized mass-religion is that it keeps half-starving people in a resigned psychological state.

All biological needs are likewise subject, at least within certain limits, to the control of psychological attitudes; and conversely it is the psychological attitude of nations and their rulers which is largely responsible for wars, famine and most types of physical deprivation. Indeed, today when total productivity and plenitude at all human levels are physically possible all over the globe, the psychological problem (and the resulting political issues) is the first one to solve. Man's need has become fundamentally psychological.

This does not mean that the college-bred psychiatrist and the psychoanalyst of our time are able to understand and formulate clearly the essential needs of humanity at the threshold of the Age of plenitude, yet frightened by the encounter with the monstrous "Dweller at the Threshold" (cf. Bulwer Lytton's *Zanoni*) which has been built by long centuries of ignorance, fear, frustration and relative spiritual failures. It means that humanity must, under penalty of death, meet and understand its basic needs; that these are primarily psychological; and that therefore a type of human individuals must arise whose main life-concentration will be in terms of human psychology—both, individual psychology and the collective psychology of permanent groups, nations and temporary crowds. This type of individuals is undoubtedly beginning to emerge. More and more an all-inclusive psychology is taking shape out of the conflict between many psychological schools, systems and techniques. But we have seen only the very beginning of it. A truly integral, as well as integrating, all-human psychology belongs still to a somewhat distant future. *Its development is an indispensable factor for world-peace.*

We need psychological understanding between nations, far more urgently than a new body of international laws. And the tragic, even ludicrous, spectacle presented by our present-day conferences of world-leaders is rooted primarily in utter psychological confusion and the failure by officials to grasp even the first elements of the national pychology of their opponents and partners. The most basic requirements for all diplomatic positions—and for *any* governmental office—should be an exhaustive study of the psychology of all nations in terms of geography, history, culture, religion and economic characteristics. Yet, we send to conferences which decide the fate of humanity representatives totally unfit psychologically to deal with the issues and needs at stake; men trained in narrow provincialistic politics; men whose backgrounds make them personally antagonistic to the persons they are supposed to befriend and convince. Psychology is at last beginning very slowly to enter the field of management and there are courses of training for "public relationship" jobs and for salesmanship— inadequate as they may be. It must renew utterly the fields of political activity and diplomacy, and transform them into the great all-inclusive realm of world-management.

The Purpose. No operation can be well managed, the purpose of which is not clear to the manager and, in the new Age of conscious and creative personality, to the co-workers engaged in this operation. Yet, our present-day leaders have no conception of the ultimate purpose of humanity or even of the nations and groups they lead, and a very scant and uncertain knowledge of what their immediate goal should be beyond the purely personal or nationalistic interests they officially represent. Purpose determines policy. A policy without a fundamental purpose is merely a crutch; it carries you along, but no one knows exactly where. Indeed the only purpose most human beings understand is to keep alive, or to become as powerful as possible. But this is instinct; not conscious and creative purpose.

The conscious realization of human purpose—individual or collective—comes to the mind of the true philosopher or to the "inner vision" of the spiritual seer and the religious prophet. It is the outcome of an impregnation of the personality by the spirit. It is a revelation, or intuitive perception, of the seedhood of humanity, Man, through the strivings and evolutionary growth of individuals and groups that are gradually being integrated in terms of this ultimate all-human seed—or, that drops away from evolution, as un-integratable elements.

The terms intuition and revelation are frowned upon by many intellectuals. They have unfortunately been misused and abused, and made to cover up psychological complexes, emotional frustrations, wild dreams or hallucinations. Philosophical intuitions which had a real spiritual core have been intellectualized into formalistic systems from which the living essence has vanished; and the "God-given Revelations" of even true Prophets have become so dogmatized and laden with incongruous psychological elements that the essential vision of the great purpose of man and the universe has been lost, first of all by the believers. Likewise the term, "authority", which has only meaning in terms of a valid and integrating revelation of all-human purpose, has become debased to the level of political autocracy or religious pontificalism.

The purpose of human life and of the universe should be evident to all men who live in conscious spontaneity of being, in a state of "openness to the universe." Any man who truly lives according to the transpersonal way must at times catch a glimpse of the spiritual purpose of all there is. The difficulty is how to express this glimpse in words, pictures or symbols; and as most men's minds lack creativity and real self-confidence in their ability to formulate superpersonal truth, their formulation of a spiritual vision usually destroys the very essence of it. Yet the purpose of man is inherent in the being and structure of man's total organism; the purpose of a nation, in the quality and rhythm of its people's life, as well as in the structure and climate of the land which supports this life. There is no mystery in these things. It is all there to be "seen" by any man with the power to "see whole."

This "holistic" realization of being is however denied to minds intent solely upon analysis, intellectual criticism, and formalistic classification. It stands thus as polar opposite to the typical "scientific" investigation of exclusivistic *classes* of data. Classes can only be established by selecting group-similarities and rejecting individual differences. Spiritual vision, however, is the direct perception of a living whole that is seen as unique, integral and endowed with a purpose with reference to the universal Whole. To see the whole in integral all-encompassing action is to realize the purpose of that whole. And he who thus sees the purpose of the whole acquires "authority".

Authority is, literally, the quality of authorship—and, secondarily, the effect of the realization of the author's identity. The Creator has authority, in so far as the creatures are concerned. And he who can realize and "see" the Creator in all creatures becomes endowed with a vicarious kind of authority. Such a power of vision makes of him an agent for (a "vicar" of) the universal Author. He can recognize this Author and His touch in whatever he does; and as a result he comes to sense the Author's purpose. In other words, he makes men see "God" everywhere. He reveals the quality and the purpose of the creative Spirit in everything, translating what he sees in terms of those common everyday experiences which the average man can understand.

Such concepts belong to the field of religion. *True religion is the path to the realization of the purpose of the creative Spirit in all organisms, individual or collective.* It should be nothing else; but, alas, it has become, in most cases, everything else except that— from the building of huge temples and interference with politics for the sake of power and privilege, to the perpetuation of psychic slavery through personal ignorance and blind faith. Yet, *whoever seeks power loses authority.* Power belongs to the realm of universal energy-substance, the Eternal Feminine (Shakti). Authority is a characteristic of spiritual consciousness. There can be no authority without spiritual consciousness (Shiva), without vision; and the man of vision is not, in most cases, the man of power—in the usual sense of the term "power." He *polarizes and gives orientation to* power. He does not manage the release and use of energy; for this belongs to the manager-scientist who deals with cause-and-effect sequences, with the serial manifestations and transformations of energy-substance.

To have authority, in the true sense of the term, is to see the meaning and purpose of spirit within every form. Form, abstractly speaking, is the expression of the purpose of spirit; but actually such a definition of "form" applies only to "archetypal," essential or (as used in later-day esthetics) "significant" form. Form in actual manifestation appears as body or object. A body is an aggregate of material particles organized according to a form; and it often happens that in the process of substantiation or materialization of the archetypal form the weight and pull of material elements distort this form— thus, thwarting or clouding the spiritual purpose of the object or organic body. When this occurs, it becomes difficult to realize what the essential purpose of the organism is. Ordinary men become confused by the distorted appearances (which may mean also the very glamour of these appearances!). Only the person who can *pierce through* these appearances and see the archetypal form can reveal the essential spiritual purpose; and by so doing he demonstrates authority.

Such demonstrations of authority are desperately needed in our modern world faced by disaster or rebirth. But this spiritual kind of authority has practically nothing in common with the concept of authoritarianism proclaimed today by political pseudo-prophets and old religious organizations, both of which seek primarily power and privilege through psychic mass-hypnosis. Authority is nothing if not a revelation of the new purpose which is established by the creative spirit at any time to meet the new need of humanity at every step of its evolutionary development. There are obviously basic human purposes which do not change throughout a historical cycle, as there is a fundamental purpose constituting the spiritual potential of the entire life of an individual person. Nevertheless, these purposes, deep in the unconscious of humanity, while undertoning the more transitory goals of the moment, cannot obliterate them.

Every moment has its creative task; every new operation of management has its purpose. This purpose must be made clear and effective at any time by men who can realize its character and meaning. We need desperately such men today, whether they appear as creative philosophers, intuitive seers or leaders of new and pure religious movements, or we shall be deluded by their Shadows; *unless* humanity consciously and with concentrated intent calls for them. Spirit answers only through conscious personalities if the need it must fill is forcefully and clearly formulated. Let us not deceive ourselves into thinking our scientists or our politicians can reveal to us man's new evolutionary goals. And let us not knock at rusty old gates if we seek creative and convincing statements of the unconscious "heart's desire" of a humanity obsessed by ghosts of scarcity and privilege. There must be new channels for new answers, new goals for new men. Only as the purpose of our human society in the making is made clear, only as we come to realize in full lucidity what we are subconsciously striving for in reaching to the core of the atom and liberating the power it contains, can we then establish valid new techniques, significant and truly organic types of planning, and coherent schedules of management.

The Planning.   Techniques alone can never save us. They are but the servants of some purpose. And if our planners and scientists are not provided with, or do not willingly respond to, some great creative purpose, then, the new techniques will serve obsolete and regressive goals; and they will destroy humanity.

We have seen what twentieth century machines, from tanks to radio, could do in the hands of the ruthless followers of the neo-tribal Nazi philosophy of life. We have seen also what the great miracle of man's controlled release of nuclear energy could do in the hands of American military and political leaders who had no long-range philosophy of life and no over-all vision beyond the reaching of immediate success. The technician's typical philosophy of life is that of not having any conscious philosophy, beside the solving of one problem after another. Likewise the typical attitude of the manager is to master difficulties of management, to overcome bottle-necks, to reach maximum efficiency at all cost. The cost is usually the spiritual fulfillment and happiness of individual persons. Thus the rule of managers would be the rule of ruthlessness and result in the sacrifice of human values and spiritual goals to productive efficiency, unless managers become the consecrated servants of noble social purposes.

There must planning; but any planning which is not completely conditioned and oriented by a valid spiritual purpose, which in turn is the answer to an evolutionary human need, either makes no sense or must prove ultimately destructive of Man. Planning is the organization of human activities and of natural or mechanical processes toward the realization of purpose. And modern science is the foundation of collective social planning because its field is the organization of a type of knowledge, the basic character of which is that it commands collective assent. It is knowledge for all and by all; knowledge that every individual accepting a definite set of collective human standards (the laws of "rigorous thinking") can verify for himself, both in its inner logical organization and in its outer applications.

World-management must therefore be "scientific"; because it must establish principles and techniques, the practical validity and effectiveness of which can be made evident to all. There can be, indeed, no global society unless it be on the basis of the common consent of a vast majority of all men; and that common consent, if it is to be a permanent and secure foundation for a world-society, cannot be subject to changing emotional mass enthusiasms, but must be established on a practically irrefutable evidence, the kind of evidence science should provide in any era. Evidence, it is true, can be altered by the acquisition of new means of knowledge, of new discoveries and of the growth of new human faculties of perception. But the change is usually quite slow. When it becomes very rapid, as it has been during the last century, a crisis of all-human social organization is unavoidable. The very foundations of collective planning are questioned, and made to crumble; and social chaos follows.

All human societies are based on some kind of planning. But while in a typical tribal society planning is collective and for the purpose of tribal fulfillment, and the type of evidence on which its techniques rest is bio-psychic and religious in character, in our modern individualistic society much of the planning is oriented toward the *goal of establishing a new basis of evidence for a universal type of human consent.*

For this reason, our modern Western society since the Renaissance has fundamentally been a revolutionary society. It is a society in which a maximum valuation has been set on the transformation of any previously accepted common basis of evidence. The more or less conscious and acknowledged goal of the intellectual elite of mankind has been to release new means of knowledge and new facts on which to establish a new type of evidence—an evidence which all men could accept—as a foundation for a global society. What a so-called "universal" religion such as Christianity could not achieve through emotional and psychic contagion, modern science is now accomplishing. Nearly all men are compelled by what seems unchallengeable evidence to accept the foundations of scientific thinking and the basic laws of science as valid. This means that a global society will become possible on the basis of this commonly accepted evidence. This means also that our modern society *will radically change*, if science retains her hold on the collective mind of humanity; for while Western society since 1600 has been a "revolutionary" society because it *sought* a new type of evidence, if now Western man is satisfied that he has *found* this universally acceptable evidence on which a global society can only be built, then he can now build such a society on a "conservative" basis.

As long as Western man sought to reach a new evolutionary phase in human history—a global society—he was driven by the need to repudiate and transform the old types of evidence: his purpose was change and overcoming. If he feels that he has reached this new evolutionary phase, that he has obtained the type of evidence which can unite the minds of all men, then, he will obviously adopt a new social attitude. He will want to build a global society on the principles and achievements of modern science.

This has been made clear to all thinking persons since the atomic bomb revealed *a new potential foundation for a global society*—or, if this foundation is not used, the inevitability of global anarchy and wholesale human destruction. It has been made particularly obvious to the scientists who worked on atomic energy and thus felt the human responsibility for what was released—against their warnings and entreaties, it has been said. They therefore have worked desperately to show the need for a world-government which alone could control safely the new atomic energy. And in a pointed article entitled *Science, nucleus of World State* (FREE WORLD, May 1946) Albert Guérard, a Stanford University professor, expresses clearly the idea that only a World Scientific Council endowed with extensive powers and resources could establish evident foundations for a new world-society. What is needed, he writes, is not "Science for Science's sake, but Science in the service of mankind." The World Scientific Council would centralize all research in a collective manner similar to that which led to the atomic bomb, would pool and release all new inventions, and "be the trustee for that 'Common Wealth,' the growing substance of the World State. A new process would be a far greater event than a treaty. . . . Diplomacy, politics, business are founded on rivalry and distrust. Even ideologies and religious faiths, in their historical formulation, divide instead of uniting mankind. Science alone completely transcends such an antagonism."

Mr. Guérard does not advocate a "political dictatorship by the Scientists, as envisaged at one time by Renan." And he adds: "Scientists are but men, and very fallible men. I want them to be free in their own domain, not to abridge our freedom. . . . I do not believe in *rank;* but I am quite willing that in a sane and 'realistic' society, scientists should outrank administrators, politicians, soldiers, business men. Outrank, not supersede. I am not ready to admit they should outrank philosophers and poets; they certainly cannot supersede them."

Similar ideas have been developed at great length by Dr. Oliver Reiser, of the Pittsburgh University, in his books on "Scientific Humanism" and especially in his work *The World Sensorium* (1945). What these men seek to promote is a new technique of social organization, a new approach to the establishment of a workable global society on the basis of the universally acceptable evidence, logical and practical, offered by the modern scientific spirit. What they seem to underestimate is the power of a dynamic spiritual purpose beyond the realm of mental objectivity and scientific achievements.

Truly, they can well say that the attainment of global peace and of a coherent organic world-society is in itself the one and only immediate purpose worth striving for, in as much as it would answer the one obvious practical need of humanity in this atomic Age. Yet the usual *scientific* approach to such a goal is one which stresses the overcoming of the immediate difficulty ahead and shuns all basic statements of human purpose and ultimate ideals. And we feel that these can no longer be left unformulated, for they alone will meet the *psychological* need of humanity as a whole. The obvious practical need of humanity today is world-organization; but as intense and poignant is the need for a new spiritual vision, for a new religious spirit.

Once more, we reach a dualism of values. Science and Religion —Planning and ultimate human Purpose—Management and Vision, from which derive basic executive policies. Today the dualism is either unclear, or expressed in terms of antagonism and warfare. A large number of human beings believe in modern science with the dogmatic fanaticism of religious devotees. Many others, who once were typical intellectuals, rush to knock at the Church's gates seeking refuge in the old formula: *Credo quia absurdum*—"I believe, because it is absurd."

Both types crave security. Both types fail to recognize the *total need* of humanity. Both types try to escape the confrontation with their own selves. Both types ignore psychology—which is harder to face and to accept than either science (its techniques and its step-by-step attainments) or religion (its emotional enthusiasm and its comforting sense of reliance upon an external God). Both types deal with collectivities and collective solutions. But the only complete solution must begin in the individual person. The integration of the personality conditions the harmony of society. An integral, harmonic psychology is the foundation of a global, harmonic society.

The road to global harmony. It cannot be trodden by man alone or by woman alone; by individualism alone, or collectivism alone;

by religion alone, or science alone; by Anglo-American democracies alone, or by a totalitarian Soviet Russia alone. Its ultimate value is not a universal God alone, or a global humanity alone; not the creative individual person alone, or the balanced and planned society alone. All opposites ever interpenetrate one another in the actual living of life; all polarities interweave their currents in the great Harmony of the Whole—the Harmony that is, both, space and the power which chords all there is in the eternal antiphony of universal life.

To see whole, to be whole, to express the wholeness of the whole whereever one is—this is the great human need. To strive after that wholeness—this is the one human goal, always new because it is eternal; because every moment of cyclic evolution presents it in a new aspect, and humanity describes it under a new name. All other goals are derivatives. To realize the harmony of the opposites in the individual and in society, to act in terms of such a harmony, to radiate the power that flows from this state of harmony: this is the task of all men alike. Some see this task as religion, others as science, still others as applied psychology. It is one task; and to-day we can give it the inclusive name of "management," for in true management the need, the purpose and the planning are encompassed.

Man is the manager of that universal power which completely pervades and surrounds him. This is his responsibility and this is his trust. Because in him all the energies of nature can reach a condition of harmony in the perfected spirit-illumined personality, man can be the microcosm of the universal Whole. As an individual, he is that Whole focused through one set of space-time values, through one particular function which it is his to discharge in harmonic companionship with all other conscious and creative individuals. And as Man, he is that Whole in complete harmonic focusing.

To realize this with the whole of one's being is to obtain inner peace. To live it in every act is to gain dynamic immortality. To radiate it through every moment is to have become God-in-Act. This is the transpersonal way: not for a Christ alone—but potentially for all men.

Epilogue

"In man, therefore, we must place our faith. . . ." Thus we wrote in the opening pages of this book. And if this entire work was nothing else but a testimony of faith in the creative powers and the universal destiny of man, it would have contributed the one thing needed in the bewildered race of mankind toward what, one day, seems a glorious new world, and the next, utter destruction.

Faith in man is the one foundation of any valid psychology; as it is of any valid social transformation. Religion as such must always fail, spiritually as well as practically, whenever it does not radiate a basic faith in man; for unless faith in man undertones faith in God the divine ideal can never become real and concrete without it becoming perverted by fear and by lust for power. But a humanism that does not acknowledge God as its creative core also must fail, because it does not realize the unity which is immanent in all human beings, however differentiated, and it envisions no essential divine purpose to establish as an ultimate of value; a purpose which becomes *spiritually evident* to all men that tread the transpersonal way.

The image of reconciliation of the opposites is "Man"; Man, the seedhood of humanity, the spiritual Identity in which all men partake; Man that is in the beginning and in the end, the alpha and omega of humanity as a whole; Man that is God's purpose enacted on earth, on continents and seas whose structures reveal, for whoever has eyes to see, the essentials of this purpose as it works itself out through individuals and through nations. In Man all individual men are divine, in as much as they act out the one purpose and the one truth of their differentiated beings. And in Man, the uni-

219

versal Harmony that is God focuses itself into total expression in space and in time.

This Man, it is God's Incarnation. Not a single event in distant times and in a distant place; but an eternal event, a progressive event, which *is,* yet forever *becomes.* In this becoming, all creative persons participate as companions, and all polarized expressions of human life and human productivity are harmonized. In this becoming of Man, creative individual freedom and purposeful necessity integrate, as man and woman integrate in the production of new human bodies and of new cultural-social structures through which a living and ever-renewed process of civilization is expressed and brought to its eventual seed-culmination.

Because we are today in the midst of a crucial phase of all-human and planetary metamorphosis ancient structures must be dissolved. New ones will arise as the new goals they must serve become clearly formulated by conscious individuals who have understanding, vision, faith and courage. These new goals are conditioned fundamentally by the shift from the state of scarcity to that of plenitude and creative human fulfillment in every conceivable realm. Today this shift is possible. What stands in the way is the lack of understanding of uneducated or, worse still, mis-educated, men. It is the inertia of mental habits and of traditional institutions. It is the fear that grips individuals and collectivities. It is their sense of inferiority, their ignorance and bewilderment long fostered by organized priesthoods and by privileged social groups; their craving for security and familiar structures, even though these might be dark with suffering and deprivation.

New goals must be envisioned. Men of vision must come; creative individuals free from ancient ghosts. No man ever truly reached that which he was unable to imagine. No man ever attained a reality in which he had no faith, and while yet attached to obsolete ideals. One cannot muddle along to victory, unless, deep in one's heart, one is certain of victory. And our present-day humanity must be victorious *as a whole;* or it will be altogether defeated. Wherefore, every conflict that seeks to split the human Whole must lead to tragedy. Every man or group that believes in the inevitability of a new world-war is a traitor to Man. Every organization, be it political or religious, that feeds this belief is an enemy of humanity and works against evolution.

What we face now is a crisis of all-human repolarization. The polarities of human life—whether in the individual, the home or society—are seeking a new level of interaction and productive interplay. Positive is no longer positive; negative is not truly negative, because neither is established in productive and co-active truth. Nothing indeed is truly what it is in relation to other things. "Right relationship" is therefore the key. Harmony is the one necessary goal, without the attainment of which there can be no attainment of any real significance. And the foundation of all efforts toward this inclusive harmony in personality and in society, is psychology —a harmonic and integrational psychology in which human depths and human roots (man's common humanity) are seen integrated with, *but also transfigured by,* the divine purpose (the "seed") in every individual and every nation, every group and every society.

These things have been stated in their several basic aspects throughout this book. The keynote it stresses is: Harmonization. The method it outlines is: The Transpersonal Way. However much the prejudiced reader might think to the contrary when confronted with this or that, to him, challenging statement, we consistently refuse to uphold one pole against the other, wherever there is a conflict between two polar and complementary personal beliefs, ideologies or social systems. We are not for individualism as against collectivism; or for collectivism as against individualism. We are not for man as against woman, or woman as against man. We do not take sides for one part of the world against another, for we refuse to see the American continent as greater than the Eurasian continent, or one race as greater than another. Greatness is a matter

of fulfillment of need and of effectively worked out spiritual purpose. And greatness must include all that is in contrast to it, if it is
to be at all great.

Men are living today through what might well be called even
now the Civil War of Man. Our one purpose and our only hope
is to express in words that have power and carry conviction whatever it may be that could help to transform this Civil War of Man
into the prelude to a Global Peace. Such a transformation must
come. It will come without further tragedy and cataclysmic war
if men are strong enough and wise enough. It may come through
the nearly total destruction of large sections of the globe, if we
let ourselves be obsessed by the ghosts of the Age of conflicts, of
power-politics and incoherent individualism.

Yet it is not enough to say that the choice is there for all mankind to make. There is a type of choice that no individual will make
until there is absolutely no other alternative, until all other roads
are blocked. To take the road to global harmony may actually mean
—however strange, this may seem!—such a kind of choice, considering the type of past, of psychology and of social compulsions
which have molded our present generations. How can we make it
clear, then, that there is no other alternative?

Scientists who feel the responsibility of having released the awesome power of the atom's core are telling us in graphic statements
that without world-control and world-government mankind is running to the abyss. Pictures of devastation are presented by all progressive writers and commentators. Radio programs dramatize the
possibility and summon the image of catastrophe. However, the
average citizen of our enlightened United States, uneasy and bewildered as he or she may be in a sort of sickening way, turns off
the radio and listens to the maudlin ineptitudes of jazz lyrics. The
average individual of this day simply cannot imagine as a concrete
reality just ahead a totally unfamiliar type of horror; even if he has
experienced something similar in the recent past. And if he *did*

imagine it, it would in most cases simply shatter his mind and personality. He would feel helpless before the event, because he has not the *creativeness* to act out a consistent personal policy in a society, the scope and complexity of which dismay him. The most he can make himself do is to support some group-activity and send letters to his congressman. As for the political or social leader, he too lacks as a rule both the creative imagination and the courage necessary to follow a line of action which would run against the inertia, the traditional habits and the personal or group interests which have led him to where he now stands.

How can men become creative and free from ghosts? How can they rise to an occasion too far ahead of their immediate perceptions to stir in them this unconscious energy of despair which often makes men faced by death accomplish incredible acts of heroism or skill?

There are only two ways, beside an actual confrontation with the obviously inescapable life-and-death alternative—which, in most cases, comes too late! Both ways mean a *radical transformation of the personal life of individuals.* The first way—the easier—is a new religion, whose mysterious collective power of psychic contagion upturns and fecundates with new vision and new energies the inner lives of many human beings, sending them if need be to joyous martyrdom. The second way—hard, slow, but permanent if successful—is the way of a spirit-conditioned, integrational psychology able to transfigure the individual and to open to him the transpersonal way to his immortality in Man. The first method is essentially collectivistic, emotional-psychic, almost obsessive in its usual results that lead to fanaticism and blind faith. The second method deals with individuals as individuals.

Today mankind is witnessing a new birth of psychology as well as a rebirth of religion. The former includes many strivings along psychological or even "occult" lines, some of which are truly spiritually transforming (in potentiality at least), others can bring only ultimate psychic confusion and self-deception through glamour or self-hypnosis. The rebirth of religion takes three forms: one is the spread of new religions, foremost among which is the Bahai Faith whose Prophets-Founders have proven, last century, by their lives and their extraordinary foresighted teachings their claim to "divine" inspiration if nothing more. The other results of this up-surge of the religious spirit, on one hand, are various attempts to instill a new vitality into older religions (Christianity and Buddhism above all), on the other hand, the return of disillusioned and weary individuals to the motherly womb of some stable and static Church that seems to offer the only bulwark against the spread of what appears to them as chaos and spiritual darkness.

Again we are confronted by two ways: a way for the individuals who seek to transform the antithetical phase of psychological egocentricity into the harmonic condition of illumined transpersonal Selfhood—and a way for the collective type of men and women who, as yet insecurely established in their individual status, need an outlet for their adolescent fervor as well as their adolescent fears, and above all need the feeling of communion with an actual tangible group of fellow human beings, and the sense of inner security which divine Revelation and God-inspired leadership can give them.

Is the one way exclusive of the other? Must there be antagonism between the individual person striving as an individual toward conscious immortality through fulfillment of his individual place and function, which establish his eternal participation in God's all-inclusive purpose, and the religious devotee seeking complete absorption in the faith a God-man founded for a collective human regeneration? We say that both ways are necessary. They complement each other, as man complements and polarizes woman, in a process of global metamorphosis.

The tragic materialization and crystallization of early Christianity was caused by the fact that the collectivistic Church built by St.

Paul and the Fathers who followed after him fought against and destroyed the individuals who in their own ways sought to incorporate the Christ-spirit in their individual lives; also, because most of these individuals did not assume their full social responsibility in a Romanized world that worshipped formalistic Law and denied the Harmony of the spirit of the Whole. This failure of *both* protagonists in the drama of all-human renewal—individuals and collectivity—need not recur in this and the following centuries. It must not recur.

If it should not take place, the spirit-arousing forces of the new humanity could act in productive interplay, and thus should inevitably triumph over all organizational crystallizations and all psychological ghosts. Such a triumph in the realm of the human mind and soul would then transfigure a struggling world-society, seeking new modes of global integration, and new patterns of productive management. For it is the spirit in man that ultimately controls all things human.

Faith in Man is faith in the creative and transforming divine spirit inherent in all human persons. This faith alone can summon the new goals which alone can orient constructively and guide steadily the infinitely complex operations of world-management. It alone can illumine the minds and feelings of men who must manage the production of social structures and cultural achievements which will make the realization of these new goals possible. This faith alone can lead egocentric individuals upon the transpersonal way, and nations jealous of their sovereign prerogatives upon the transnational way. And the center of that faith is the readiness to serve.

To serve God in concrete reality is to serve Man in the realization of the Holy Spirit that is truth and understanding. For man, understood in essential reality, is God's purpose—God-in-Act. And every individual person who seeks to achieve immortality in Man, is inevitably treading the path of divine Sonship. For Man is God incorporated.

And let no one call this "mysticism" and rush busily, with a shrug of the shoulders, to his "realistic" task of saving democracy *via* the atomic bomb, or of saving humanity *from* the atomic bomb! Everything depends upon man. Everything in man rests upon psychological attitudes and psychological decisions. Spirituality is a psychological attitude. Service, whether of God or Man, stems from psychological decisions. It is time for men, individually and collectively, to realize that it is psychological decisions that count most. Ideas rule the world. And a Christ still lives in the hearts and souls of countless millions, while a deluded individual who allowed the ghost of Caesar to control his mind has nothing perhaps to offer his God save ignominous death and a world-cataclysm that killed or wrecked untold millions of lives.

The Roman Empire was necessary for the spread of Christianity, because "form" is always necessary for the spread of any creative impulse released from the spirit. Alas! form but too often overpowers spirit. Rome triumphed over Christ, by organizing Christianity according to the ways of Rome. That this may not happen again all men of vision and courage must unite in the sacred companionship of the new Logos, and give their all in the service of these new goals which, as men vitally understand their meaning and work in utter concentration and self-consecration toward their realization, alone will transfigure humanity. Humanity needs to be transfigured, not to be saved. There is no death that the spirit in man cannot overcome, if men become agents for the spirit.

Index